Selection of Hotels and Restaurants

plus section on Points of Excursion

Where do you start? Choosing a hotel or restaurant in a place you're not familiar with can be daunting. To help you find your way amid the bewildering variety, we have made a selection from the *Red Guide to Benelux 1989* published by Michelin, the recognized authority on gastronomy and accommodation throughout Europe.

Our own Berlitz criteria have been price and location. In the hotel section, for a double room with bath and breakfast, Higher-priced means above BF 5,000, Medium-priced BF 3,000–5,000, Lower-priced below BF 3,000. As to restaurants, for a meal consisting of a starter, a main course and a dessert, Higher-priced means above BF 1,700, Medium-priced BF 1,100–1,700, Lower-priced below BF 1,100. For points of excursion outside Brussels, however, to avoid confusion of detail, we have simply replaced after each entry the three categories with $$$ for Higher-priced, $$ for Medium-priced and $ for Lower-priced. Special features where applicable, plus regular closing days are also given. As a general rule many Brussels restaurants are closed end July–mid-August. For hotels and restaurants, both a check to make certain that they are open and advance reservations are advisable. In Belgium, hotel and restaurant prices include service and taxes.

For a wider choice of hotels and restaurants, we strongly recommend you obtain the authoritative Michelin *Red Guide to Benelux,* which gives a comprehensive and reliable picture of the situation throughout these countries.

Brussels

HOTELS

HIGHER-PRICED
(above BF 5,000)

Amigo
rue Amigo 1
1000 Brussels
Tel. 5115910; tlx. 21618
Beautifully furnished interior.

Brussels Europa Hotel
rue de la Loi 107
1040 Brussels
Tel. 2301333; tlx. 25121

Brussels-Sheraton Towers
place Rogier 3
1210 Brussels
Tel. 2193400; tlx. 26887
Indoor swimming pool.

Hilton International Brussels
bd Waterloo 38
1000 Brussels
Tel. 5138877; tlx. 22744
*Maison du Bœuf restaurant and
Plein-Ciel restaurant on 27th floor
with view over the city.*

Hyatt Regency Brussels
rue Royale 250
1210 Brussels
Tel. 2171234; tlx. 61871

Jolly H. Atlanta
bd A.-Max 7
1000 Brussels
Tel. 2170120; tlx. 21475
No restaurant.

Mayfair
av. Louise 381
1050 Brussels
Tel. 6499800; tlx. 24821

Métropole
place de Brouckère 31
1000 Brussels
Tel. 2172300; tlx. 21234
Elegant restaurant.

President World Trade Center
bd Emile Jacqmain 180
1210 Brussels
Tel. 2172020; tlx. 21066

Royal Windsor Hotel
rue Duquesnoy 5
1000 Brussels
Tel. 5114215; tlx. 62905
Les 4 Saisons restaurant.

Stéphanie
av. Louise 91
1050 Brussels
Tel. 5390240; tlx. 25558
Indoor swimming pool.

Outskirts of Brussels

Holiday Inn
Holidaystraat 7
1920 Diegem
Tel. 7205865; tlx. 24285
*Indoor swimming pool,
hotel tennis court.*

Sofitel
Bessenveldstraat 15
1920 Diegem
Tel. 7251160; tlx. 26595
Indoor swimming pool, garden.

MEDIUM-PRICED
(BF 3,000–5,000)

L'Agenda
rue Florence 6
1050 Brussels
Tel. 5390031; tlx. 63947
No restaurant.

Alfa Louise
rue Blanche 4
1050 Brussels
Tel. 5379210; tlx. 62434
No restaurant.

Archimède
rue Archimède 22
1040 Brussels
Tel. 2310909; tlx. 20420
No restaurant.

Arenberg
rue d'Assaut 15
1000 Brussels
Tel. 5110770; tlx. 25660

Bedford
rue Midi 135
1000 Brussels
Tel. 5127840; tlx. 24059

Brussels
av. Louise 315
1050 Brussels
Tel. 6402415; tlx. 25075
No restaurant.

La Cascade
rue Source 14
1060 Brussels
Tel. 5388830; tlx. 26637
No restaurant.

Chambord
rue Namur 82
1000 Brussels
Tel. 5134119; tlx. 20373
No restaurant.

Chelton
rue Véronèse 48
1040 Brussels
Tel. 7364095; tlx. 64253
No restaurant.

County House
Square des Héros 2
1180 Brussels
Tel. 3754420; tlx. 22392

Delta
chaussée de Charleroi 17
1060 Brussels
Tel. 5390160; tlx. 63225

Euro-flat
bd Charlemagne 50
1040 Brussels
Tel. 2300010; tlx. 21120
No restaurant.

New Hotel Siru
place Rogier 1
1210 Brussels
Tel. 2177580; tlx. 21722
Original interior decor.

Président Nord
bd A.-Max 107
1000 Brussels
Tel. 2190060; tlx. 61417
No restaurant.

Outskirts of Brussels

Novotel
Olmenstraat
1920 Diegem
Tel. 7205830; tlx. 26751
Heated outdoor swimming pool.

LOWER-PRICED
(below BF 3,000)

Ambassade
place des Barricades 1 a
1000 Brussels
Tel. 2182061; tlx. 62358
No restaurant.

Argus
rue Capitaine Crespel 6
1050 Brussels
Tel. 5140770; tlx. 29393
No restaurant.

Ascot
place Loix 1
1060 Brussels
Tel. 5388835; tlx. 25010
No restaurant.

Lambermont
bd Lambermont 322
1030 Brussels
Tel. 2425595; tlx. 62220
No restaurant.

Leopold
rue Luxembourg 35
1040 Brussels
Tel. 5111828; tlx. 62804

Vendôme
bd A.-Max. 98
1000 Brussels
Tel. 2180070; tlx. 64460
No restaurant.

Outskirts of Brussels

Centrum Hotel du Centre
Steenweg op Ukkel 11
1650 Beersel
Tel. 3762615
Quiet hotel.

RESTAURANTS

HIGHER-PRICED
(above BF 1,700)

Béarnais
bd Mettewie 318
1080 Brussels
Tel. 5231151
Closed Sunday and Monday evening.

Bernard
rue Namur 93
1000 Brussels
Tel. 5128821
Seafood specialities. Closed Sunday and Monday evening.

Bruneau
av. Broustin 73
1080 Brussels
Tel. 4276978
Elegant classic restaurant. Superb cuisine. Closed Tuesday evening and Wednesday.

Comme Chez Soi
place Rouppe 23
1000 Brussels
Tel. 5122921
Superb cuisine. Reservation essential. Closed Sunday and Monday. Belle Epoque atmosphere in a decor by Horta.

La Cravache d'Or
place A.-Leemans 10
1050 Brussels
Tel. 5383746
Notably good cuisine. Closed Saturday lunchtime. Reservation essential.

Dupont
av. Vital-Riethuisen 46
1080 Brussels
Tel. 4275450
Elegant classic restaurant. Excellent cuisine. Closed Monday and Tuesday.

L'Ecailler du Palais Royal
rue Bodenbroek 18
1000 Brussels
Tel. 5128751
Seafood restaurant. Excellent cuisine. Reservation essential. Closed Sunday.

Eddie Van Maele
chaussée Romaine 964
1810 Brussels
Tel. 4606145
Notably good cuisine. Flower-filled terrace and garden. Reservation essential. Closed Saturday lunchtime, Sunday and Monday.

Le Fronton Basque
chaussée de Waterloo 361
1060 Brussels
Tel. 5372118
Oysters and seafood specialities. Closed Tuesday.

Gesuino
rue Fiennes 3
1070 Brussels
Tel. 5215163
Elegant restaurant. Notably good Italian cuisine. Closed Saturday and Sunday.

Maison du Cygne
Grand'Place 9
1000 Brussels
Tel. 5118244
Beautiful old building with elegant interior. Excellent cuisine. Closed Saturday lunchtime and Sunday.

Mon Manège à Toi
rue Neerveld 1
1200 Brussels
Tel. 7700238
In a villa with a flower-filled garden. Excellent cuisine. Closed Saturday and Sunday.

L'Oasis
place Marie-José 9
1050 Brussels
Tel. 6484545
Elegant restaurant. Pavilion looking onto garden. Notably good cuisine. Closed Saturday lunchtime and Sunday.

Sirène d'Or
place Ste-Catherine 1a
1000 Brussels
Tel. 5135198
Notably good cuisine. Closed Sunday and Monday.

Trente rue de la Paille
rue Paille 30
1000 Brussels
Tel. 5120715
*Notably good cuisine. Closed
Saturday and Sunday.*

Villa d'Este
rue Etoile 142
1180 Brussels
Tel. 3778646
*Notably good cuisine. Outdoor
dining. Closed Sunday evening
and Monday.*

Villa Lorraine
av. Vivier-d'Oie 75
1180 Brussels
Tel. 3743163
*Elegant classic restaurant. Excel-
lent cuisine. Reservation desirable.
Closed Sunday.*

Outskirts of Brussels

Barbizon
Welriekendedreef 95
1900 Overijse
Tel. 6570462
*Notably good cuisine. Outdoor
dining. Reservation essential.
Closed Tuesday and Wednesday.*

Hostellerie Bellemolen
Stationstraat 11
1705 Essene
Tel. 666238
*12th-century mill, furnished with
taste. Notably good cuisine. Closed
Sunday evening and Monday.*

Romeyer
chaussée de Groenendaal 109
1990 Hoeilaart
Tel. 6570581
*Superb cuisine. Stately home
(beautiful building). View of
garden and private lake. Closed
Sunday evening and Monday.*

MEDIUM-PRICED
(BF 1,100–1,700)

Aux Armes de Bruxelles
rue Bouchers 13
1000 Brussels
Tel. 5115598
*Typical Brussels atmosphere.
Open till 11 p.m. Closed Monday.*

Astrid "Chez Pierrot"
rue de la Presse 21
1000 Brussels
Tel. 2173831
Closed Sunday.

Les Baguettes Impériales
av. J. Sobieski 70
1020 Brussels
Tel. 4796732
*Notably good Vietnamese cuisine.
Exotic setting. Closed Sunday
evening and Tuesday.*

Le Barolo
av. de Laeken 57
1090 Brussels
Tel. 4254576
*Italian cuisine. Outdoor dining.
Closed Tuesday and Wednesday.*

La Belle Maraîchère
place Ste-Catherine 11
1000 Brussels
Tel. 5129759
Notably good cuisine. Closed Wednesday and Thursday.

Au Beurre Blanc
rue Faucon 2a
1000 Brussels
Tel. 5130111
Notably good cuisine. Closed Saturday and Sunday.

Le Calvados
av. de Fré 182
1180 Brussels
Tel. 3747098
1900s decor. Outdoor dining. Closed Sunday.

Au Cheval Marin
Marché-aux-Porcs 25
1000 Brussels
Tel. 5130287
Period decor. Closed Sunday evening.

François
quai aux Briques 2
1000 Brussels
Tel. 5116089
Notably good cuisine. Seafood. Closed Monday.

La Grignotière
chaussée de Wavre 2041
1160 Brussels
Tel. 6728185
Notably good cuisine. Reservation essential. Closed Sunday and Monday.

La Réserve
chaussée de Ninove 675
1080 Brussels
Tel. 5222653
Closed Saturday lunchtime, Monday evening and Tuesday.

La Salade Folle
av. Jules Dujardin 9
1150 Brussels
Tel. 7701961
Buffet and grill. Outdoor dining. Closed Sunday evening and Monday.

Le Sermon
av. Jacques-Sermon 91
1090 Brussels
Tel. 4268935
Notably good cuisine. Closed Sunday and Monday.

La Table d'Or
rue Fourche 50
1000 Brussels
Tel. 2174700
Open until 11 p.m. Closed Saturday and Sunday lunchtime.

De Ultieme Hallucinatie
rue Royale 316
1210 Brussels
Tel. 2170614
Art nouveau interior. Closed Saturday lunchtime and Sunday.

Le Val Joli
rue Leestbeek 16
1820 Brussels
Tel. 4606543
Terrace garden. Outdoor dining. Closed Monday and Tuesday.

LOWER-PRICED
(below BF 1,100)

Adrienne Atomium
Parc Expositions
1020 Brussels
Tel. 4783000
Hors d'œuvre. View. Closed Sunday.

Les Cadets de Gascogne
rue Florence 26
1050 Brussels
Tel. 5384640
Outdoor dining. Closed Saturday lunchtime and Sunday.

Le Citron Vert
av. H. Conscience 242
1140 Brussels
Tel. 2411257
Closed Tuesday.

Comme Ça
rue Châtelain 61
1050 Brussels
Tel. 6496290
*Closed Sunday,
Monday evening.*

Le Gigotin
rue Stevin 102
1040 Brussels
Tel. 2303091
Outdoor dining. Closed Saturday and Sunday.

Henri Ier
av. de Messidor 181
1180 Brussels
Tel. 3452629

Old inn. Grill. Outdoor dining. Closed Monday.

De Hoef
rue Edith-Cavell 218
1180 Brussels
Tel. 3743417
17th-century inn. Grill. Outdoor dining.

't Kelderke
Grand'Place 15
1000 Brussels
Tel. 5137344
Typical Brussels atmosphere. Open till 2 a.m.

Chez Léon
rue Bouchers 18
1000 Brussels
Tel. 5111415
Typical Brussels atmosphere. Open until midnight. Mussels a speciality when in season.

La Madonette
rue Eglise 92
1150 Brussels
Tel. 7310298
Outdoor dining. Closed Tuesday lunchtime and Monday.

Yser
rue Edimbourg 9
1050 Brussels
Tel. 5117459
Mussels a speciality when in season. Closed Sunday evening and Monday.

Points of Excursion

ANTWERP

Hotels

Alfa Congress $$
Plantin en Moretuslei 136
2018 Antwerp
Tel. (03) 2353000; tlx. 31959

Alfa De Keyser $$$
De Keyserlei 66
2018 Antwerp
Tel. (03) 2340135; tlx. 34219

Alfa Theater $$
Arenbergstraat 30
2000 Antwerp
Tel. (03) 2311720; tlx. 33910

Restaurants

't Fornuis $$$
Reyndersstraat 24
2000 Antwerp
Tel. (03) 2336270
Notably good cuisine. Country-style restaurant. Closed Saturday and Sunday.

Fourchette $
Schuttershofstraat 28
2000 Antwerp
Tel. (03) 2313335
Closed Saturday lunchtime, Sunday and Monday.

Koperen Ketel $$
Wiegstraat 5
2000 Antwerp
Tel. (03) 2331274
Closed Saturday lunchtime and Sunday.

Manoir $$
Everdijstraat 13
2000 Antwerp
Tel. (03) 2327697
Interesting woodwork interior. Closed Wednesday.

Panaché $
Statiestr. 17
2018 Antwerp
Tel. (03) 2326905
Open until 1.30 a.m. Snacks available.

La Pérouse $$$
Steenplein
2000 Antwerp
Tel. (03) 2323528
Excellent cuisine. View. On a moored boat. Closed Sunday and Monday. Reservation essential.

Rooden-Hoed $$
Oude Koornmarkt 25
2000 Antwerp
Tel. (03) 2332844
Typical Antwerp atmosphere. Mussels a speciality in season. Closed Wednesday and Thursday.

Sir Anthony Van Dijck $$$
Oude Koornmarkt 16
2000 Antwerp
Tel. (03) 2316170

*Notably good cuisine. Situated in
a narrow 16th-century alleyway.
Interior furnished with taste.
Closed Saturday and Sunday.*

Vateli $$
Kipdorpvest 50
2000 Antwerp
Tel. (03) 2331781
*Notably good cuisine. Classic
restaurant. Closed Sunday and
Monday.*

BLANKENBERGE

Hotels

Azaert $$
Molenstraat 31
8370 Blankenberge
Tel. (050) 411599
Tastefully arranged interior.

Commerce $
Weststraat 64
8370 Blankenberge
Tel. (050) 411430

Idéal $
Zeedijk 244
8370 Blankenberge
Tel. (050) 411691
*Indoor swimming pool. Outdoor
dining.*

Restaurants

Joinville $
J. de Troozlaan 5
8370 Blankenberge
Tel. (050) 412269
*Closed Wednesday evening and
Thursday.*

BRUGES

Hotels

Adornes $$
St-Annarei 26
8000 Bruges
Tel. (050) 341336
*View. Tastefully arranged
interior. Vaulted cellar.
No restaurant.*

Anselmus $
Ridderstraat 15
8000 Bruges
Tel. (050) 341374
No restaurant.

Biskajer $$
Biskajersplein 4
8000 Bruges
Tel. (050) 341506; tlx. 81874
No restaurant. Quiet hotel.

Bourgoensch Hof $$
Wollestraat 39
8000 Bruges
Tel. (050) 331645; tlx. 26937
*Quiet hotel. View over the
canals and old Flemish houses.
No restaurant.*

Bryghia $$
Oosterlingenplein 4
8000 Bruges
Tel. (050) 338059
No restaurant.

Jacobs $
Baliestraat 1
8000 Bruges
Tel. (050) 339831; tlx. 81693
Quiet hotel. No restaurant.

Novotel $$
Chartreuseweg 20
8200 Bruges
Tel. (050) 382851; tlx. 81507
Outdoor dining. Outdoor swimming pool. Garden.

Orangerie $$$
Karthuizerinnestraat 10
8000 Bruges
Tel. (050) 341649; tlx. 82443
Quiet hotel. Ancient building with well arranged interior. No restaurant.

Oud Huis Amsterdam $$$
Spiegelrei 3
8000 Bruges
Tel. (050) 341810; tlx. 83121
Quiet hotel. View. 17th-century dwelling, in former Dutch trading-house.

Prinsenhof $$
Ontvangersstraat 9
8000 Bruges
Tel. (050) 342690; tlx. 81315
Quiet hotel. Tastefully arranged interior. No restaurant.

Ter Duinen $
Langerei 52
8000 Bruges
Tel. (050) 330437
No restaurant.

Restaurants

Boudewijn I $
't Zand 21
8000 Bruges
Tel. (050) 336962; tlx. 81163
Closed Tuesday.

Eglantier $$
Ezelstraat 120
8000 Bruges
Tel. (050) 332946
Closed Sunday evening and Monday.

Hermitage $$
Ezelstraat 18
8000 Bruges
Tel. (050) 344173
Closed Tuesday evening, Wednesday and Sunday evening.

De Karmeliet $$$
Jeruzalemstraat 1
8000 Bruges
Tel. (050) 338259
Excellent cuisine. Closed Sunday evening and Monday.

De Postiljon $
Katelijnestraat 3
8000 Bruges
Tel. (050) 335616
Closed Sunday evening and Tuesday.

Weinebrugge $$$
Koning Albertlaan 242
8200 Bruges
Tel. (050) 384440
Excellent cuisine. Closed Wednesday and Thursday. Reservation essential at the weekend.

De Witte Poorte $$$
Jan Van Eyckplein 6
8000 Bruges
Tel. (050) 330883; tlx. 82232

Notably good cuisine. Restaurant situated in a vaulted former warehouse. Garden. Closed Sunday and Monday.

De Zilveren Pauw $$
Zilverstraat 41
8000 Bruges
Tel. (050) 335566
Outdoor dining. Belle Epoque interior. Patio. Closed Tuesday evening and Wednesday.

GHENT

Hotels

Alfa Flanders Hotel $$
Koning Albertlaan 121
9000 Ghent
Tel. (091) 226065; tlx. 12404
Elegant, contemporary interior.

Europahotel $
Gordunakaai 59
9000 Ghent
Tel. (091) 226071; tlx. 11547

Novotel Gent Centrum $$
Gouden Leeuwplein 5
9000 Ghent
Tel. (091) 242230; tlx. 11400
Outdoor swimming pool.

St. Jorishof $$
Botermarkt 2
9000 Ghent
Tel. (091) 242424; tlx. 12738
With restaurant in a 13th-century Flemish-style room.

Restaurants

Apicius $$$
Maurice Maeterlinckstraat 8
9000 Ghent
Tel. (091) 224600
Excellent cuisine. Closed Saturday lunchtime and Sunday.

Aton $
De Pintelaan 86
9000 Ghent
Tel. (091) 216926
Closed Sunday evening and Monday evening.

Het Cooremetershuys $$
Graslei 12
9000 Ghent
Tel. (091) 234971
Period setting. Closed Sunday.

Horse Shoe $$$
Lievekaai 12
9000 Ghent
Tel. (091) 235517
Country-style decor. Closed Saturday and Sunday.

Karel De Stoute $$
Vrouwebroersstraat 5
9000 Ghent
Tel. (091) 241735
Outdoor dining. Closed Saturday lunchtime and Sunday.

Patijntje $$
Gordunakaai 91
9000 Ghent
Tel. (091) 223273
Closed Sunday and Monday.

Ter Toren $$
Sint Bernadettestraat 626
9000 Ghent
Tel. (091) 511129
Outdoor dining in shady park.
Closed Sunday evening, Monday
and Wednesday evening.

KNOKKE-HEIST

Albert-Strand

Hotels

Astoria $
Zeedijk 550
8300 Knokke-Heist
Tel. (050) 601457
View.

La Réserve $$$
Elisabethlaan 160
8300 Knokke-Heist
Tel. (050) 610606; tlx. 81657
Outdoor dining. Terrace facing
the lake. Indoor swimming pool.
Hotel tennis court.

Restaurants

Esmeralda $$
J. Nellenslaan 161
8300 Knokke-Heist
Tel. (050) 603366
Closed Tuesday.

Les Flots Bleus $
Zeedijk 538
8300 Knokke-Heist
Tel. (050) 602710
Closed Thursday.

Duinbergen

Hotels

Chenoy Manor $$
Engelsestraat 18
8390 Heist
Tel. (050) 515529
Quiet hotel. View. Tastefully
arranged interior. No restaurant.

Monterey $$
Bocheldreef 4
8390 Heist
Tel. (050) 515865
Quiet hotel. No restaurant. View.
Transformed villa.

Les Pingouins $
Duinendreef 52
8390 Heist
Tel. (050) 513340
Outdoor dining. Hotel tennis
court. Garden.

Restaurants

Auberge Pré Feuillet $
Leeuwerikenlaan 5
8390 Heist
Tel. (050) 511066
View. Outdoor dining.

Heist

Hotels

Bristol $
Zeedijk 291
8390 Heist
Tel. (050) 511220
View.

Restaurants

Old Fisher $$
Heldenplein 33
8390 Heist
Tel. (050) 51114
Seafood.

Knokke

Hotels

Malibu $$
Kustlaan 43
8300 Knocke-Heist
Tel. (050) 611803
No restaurant.

Restaurants

Ambassador $$$
Van Bunnenplein 20
8300 Knocke-Heist
Tel. (050) 601796
*Closed Wednesday evening and
Thursday.*

Hippocampus $$
Kragendijk 188
8300 Knocke-Heist
Tel. (050) 604570
*Typical Flemish homestead.
Closed Wednesday. View.*

Panier d'Or $$
Zeedijk 659
8300 Knocke-Heist
Tel. (050) 603189
View. Closed Monday.

P'tit Bedon $
Zeedijk 672
3800 Knocke-Heist
Tel. (050) 600664
*Outdoor dining. Grill. Closed
Wednesday.*

Zoute

Hotels

Auberge St. Pol $$
Bronlaan 23
8300 Knokke-Heist
Tel. (050) 601521
Outdoor dining. Terrace.

Duc de Bourgogne – Golf H.
Zoutelaan 175
8300 Knokke-Heist
Tel. 611614; tlx. 81273
Outdoor dining. Terrace.

Lugano et Manoir du Dragon $$
Villapad 14
8300 Knokke-Heist
Tel. (050) 610471
*Outdoor dining. Garden. Quiet
hotel, decorated with taste. View.*

Victoria $
Golvenstraat 6
8300 Knokke-Heist
Tel. (050) 601420
No restaurant.

Restaurants

Gasthof Katelijne $$
Kustlaan 166
8300 Knokke-Heist
Tel. (050) 601216
*Outdoor dining. Country-style inn
with view. Terrace.*

Marie Siska $
Zoutelaan 177
8300 Knokke-Heist
Tel. (050) 601764
Outdoor dining.

OSTEND

Hotels

Andromeda $$
Kursaal Westhelling 5
8400 Ostend
Tel. (059) 806611; tlx. 82056
View. Outdoor dining. Outdoor swimming pool.

Burlington $
Kapellestraat 90
8400 Ostend
Tel. (059) 701552; tlx. 82340
With taverne-restaurant.

Impérial $$
Van Iseghemlaan 76
8400 Ostend
Tel. (059) 806767; tlx. 81167

Die Prince $
Albert-I Promenade 41
8400 Ostend
Tel. (059) 706507; tlx. 81283
No restaurant. View.

Strand Hotel $
Visserskaai 1
8400 Ostend
Tel. (059) 703383; tlx. 81357
View. Elegant restaurant.

Restaurants

La Crevette $
Visserskaai 46
8400 Ostend
Tel. (059) 702130
Outdoor dining.

Le Grillon $
Visserskaai 31
8400 Ostend
Tel. (059) 706063
Closed Thursday.

Lusitania $$
Visserskaai 35
8400 Ostend
Tel. (059) 701765
View. Collection of paintings.

WATERLOO

Restaurants

Maison du Seigneur $$$
chaussée de Tervuren 389
1410 Waterloo
Tel. (02) 3540750
Outdoor dining. Brabant-style, 17th-century farm. Closed Monday and Tuesday.

Sphinx $
chaussée de Tervuren 178
1410 Waterloo
Tel. (02) 3548643
Outdoor dining. Closed Tuesday evening and Wednesday.

BERLITZ®

BRUSSELS

1990/1991 Edition

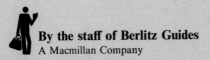

By the staff of Berlitz Guides
A Macmillan Company

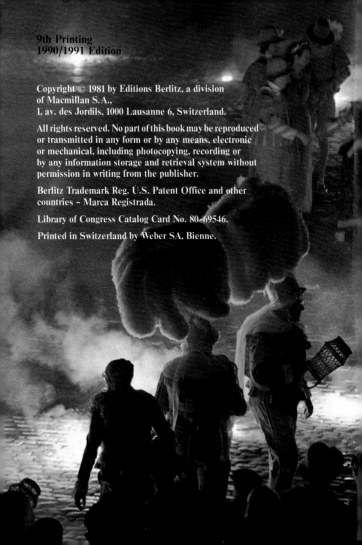

How to use our guide

- All the practical information, hints and tips that you will need before and during the trip start on page 101.

- For general background, see the sections The City and the People, p. 6, and A Brief History, p. 12.

- All the sights to see are listed between pages 26 and 54, with suggestions for daytrips and excursions from Brussels on pages 55 to 84. Our own choice of sights most highly recommended is pinpointed by the Berlitz traveller symbol.

- Entertainment, nightlife and all other leisure activities are described between pages 84 and 93, while information on restaurants and cuisine is to be found on pages 94 to 100.

- Finally, there is an index at the back of the book, pp. 126–128.

Although we make every effort to ensure the accuracy of all the information in this book, changes occur incessantly. We cannot therefore take responsibility for facts, prices, addresses and circumstances in general that are constantly subject to alteration. Our guides are updated on a regular basis as we reprint, and we are always grateful to readers who let us know of any errors, changes or serious omissions they come across.

Text: Jack Altman
Photography: Claude Huber
Layout: Doris Haldemann
Special thanks to David Pulman for his collaboration on this guide. We are also grateful to the Brussels Tourist Office and to Claire Teeuwissen for their assistance.
Cartography: 🔴 Falk-Verlag, Hamburg.

Contents

Cover picture: Guildhalls on the Grand-Place
Photo, pp. 2–3: Ommegang

The City and the People

The people of Brussels long ago resolved, come what may, to have a good time. Their determination is contagious. Out of a city that, for most of its history, was capital of nothing has grown a capital of Europe, of the Atlantic alliance, of Western capitalism and, of course, of Belgium. The mixture of roles and the

invasion of hordes of bureaucrats, Eurocrats, brigadier-generals, lawyers, businessmen and property developers might have washed away the city's identity in a sea of paper, ink and computer cards. But Brussels has known quite a few invaders in its time—Roman legions, Spanish Inquisitors, the armies of the Habsburgs, Napoleon, the Kaiser and Hitler. And somehow the people's fierce independence, robust sense of humour and, above

all, their overriding scepticism prevail. Brussels simply cocks its snoot, and you take it or leave it. On its own terms.

If you agree to see Brussels as the natives do, as a town of lively old-fashioned working-class districts and elegant bourgeois neighbourhoods tucked away behind the business-men's skyscrapers, a town of fine restaurants and lusty taverns, fascinating museums and beautiful parks, you'll find a place of distinctive personality and considerable pleasure.

On a continent where most capitals' major landmarks are cathedrals or royal palaces, it's surely significant that Brussels'

Brussels is good beer, good cheer and good fellowship and the gleaming industrial progress symbolized by the soaring stainless steel Atomium.

glories are secular and municipal—the magnificent town hall and the trade guildhalls grouped around the Grand-Place. Brussels is the triumphal monument of its bourgeois prosperity snatched repeatedly from the ravages of bombardment, revolution and foreign occupation.

The people's profoundly Catholic tradition is comfortably coupled with an exuberantly profane attitude to life. There's nothing fragile, delicate or introverted about a constitution that not only withstands, but even thrives on a diet of beer, mussels and *frites*. That's the workaday menu; life à la carte on high days and holidays exhibits a culinary finesse and inventiveness that concedes nothing to the French. In addition, the town's prosperity permits all the elegance of the boutiques along the Avenue Louise and the Chaussée de Waterloo as well as the boisterous bustle of the Place de Brouckère and Boulevard Anspach.

High days and holidays have always played a dominant role in the life of this city, a taste for bread and circuses introduced by the medieval dukes of Burgundy. The people of Brussels love dressing up in costumes from all the ages of their long history—the guilds of the Middle Ages, the aristocracy of the Renaissance —everything is grist to their merry mill. There's something exquisite about a chubby, potato-nosed, red-faced Fleming sporting the ruff, doublet and breeches of a Spanish hidalgo, or a slightly embarrassed Walloon bank-manager donning the rough linen shirt, leather apron and boots of some ancestral leatherworker who distinguished himself in the guilds. Many of the festivals and processions are of course derived from religious holidays, but the most spectacular seem to be those, purely secular, which started with the citizenry proudly parading before a visiting ruler during a Joyeuse Entrée or Ommegang.

Yes, Brussels is bilingual. While the rest of Belgium's nearly 10 million inhabitants are divided into Dutch-speaking Flemings in the northern region (57 per cent of the population) and French-speaking Walloons in the south (33 per cent), the capital (10 per cent)

International organizations have brought the city great prosperity reflected along the Avenue Louise.

manages its own version of both. And in the working-class neighbourhoods a *patois* has evolved of Flemish mixed with French, a smattering of Spanish and even a couple of words of Hebrew. The street signs and public notices appear in both languages in Brussels *(Bruxelles/Brussel)*, but the people's written language is overwhelmingly French—much to the chagrin of Flemish leaders who would like to see bilingualism more forcefully encouraged.

Those who like generalizations say the Walloons are talkative and perpetual malcontents—like the French?—and the Flemings ponderous and mystical—like the Dutch? But as everybody knows, generalizations are generally false. Apart from a handful of extremists, there are few Flemings who would like to be Dutch or Walloons who want to be French.

The national slogan is *"L'union fait la force"* (Union brings strength) and they're still working on it. The Flemish-Walloon squabbles continue, but some reconciliation is to be found in Brussels' official bilingualism and new international status. The various institutions of the European Community, NATO and associated

organisms and private international companies have brought some 230,000 foreigners to Brussels, nearly one in four of the total population.

They find Brussels an airy capital of over 1 million people. Only the town centre is actually named "Brussels", the rest of the city is made up of 18 autonomous boroughs with their own mayors, police forces and fire departments. And each has a distinctive identity marked by its liberal, conser-

Belgian art has often sought to escape the banality of everyday life with other-worldly surrealism—from Bosch to this mural by Delvaux.

vative or socialist, Fleming or Walloon, working-class or bourgeois tradition. Since the 19th century, urban planning has thrust wide avenues from the dense city centre—shaped like a pressing-iron—out to the spacious exterior boulevards circling the periphery. The parks are innumerable, magnificent and much frequen-

ted. Brussels is a town that breathes.

The gigantic Palais de Justice, symbol of Belgium's 19th-century imperial self-assertion finds its counterweight in the skyscrapers of the multinational empires of today. The museums proudly display the glories of old Flemish masters, but the strong and solid sub- **11** jects of those paintings, peasant and burgher alike, can still be seen wandering the narrow backstreets off the Grand-Place. Yet apart from the festive set-pieces of historical pageantry, the city is very much a town of the 20th century, accepting the present in a matter-of-fact way with few nostalgic glances to the past. The symbol of Brussels today is definitely the Atomium, the huge molecular model of nine aluminium-covered steel spheres, left over from the 1958 World's Fair. Its slogan was *"Bâtir le monde pour l'homme"* (Building the world for mankind), with the accent on building.

Brussels is the town of the unbelievably good-natured comic-strip adventurer Tintin and, briefly and not too happily, it was home to the bittersweet balladeer Jacques Brel. But, most of all, it's the town of wise old Pieter Brueghel. His masterpiece, *The Fall of Icarus*, hangs in the Musées Royaux des Beaux-Arts as a delightful illustration of Brussels' affirmative spirit: a man goes on ploughing his field and a shepherd dreamily tends his flock while poor old Icarus, who flew too near the sun and melted his wings, falls unnoticed into the sea. Life goes on.

A Brief History

Julius Caesar came to Belgium in 57 B.C., saw it and, after a lot of trouble with what he said were "the bravest of all the peoples of Gaul", conquered it. But he never went to Brussels. It was outside the main network of Roman roads, though by the evidence of a few bronzes, coins and funeral urns found along the Chaussée de Haecht and the Rue Haute, a few dignitaries and officers seemed to have built villas in the area.

During the 450 years of Roman rule, the Belgae of the southern region became heavily Latinized while the north was left to the Germanic tribes, creating the division which led to the subsequent conflicts between French-speaking Walloons and Dutch-speaking Flemings.

Brussels, in the middle of these two regions, was first heard of in A.D. 695, when the bishop of Cambrai fell ill there during a tour of his diocese. Brosella it was called then but was later known variously as Brucella, Bruocsella, Bruohsella, Bruesella and Borsella, with as many different meanings suggested by historians—from "dwelling near the bridge" to "stork's nest"—though the most generally accepted seems to be "dwelling in the marshes". This supposedly refers to the three swampy islands in the (now paved-over) River Senne on which the town was built.

The Middle Ages

The foundation of the city proper dates back officially to 979 when Charles de Lotharingie, brother of King Lothaire of France, erected a fortress there.

In the following century the town began to look more like a town when Count Lambert II of Louvain built a new castle on the Coudenberg heights (today's Place Royale), surrounded by houses inside a walled-in compound. These dwellings were reserved for the count's knights and administrators, while less fortunate artisans and peasants were left unprotected outside the ramparts, laying the foundations for the long struggle between the city's haves and have-nots.

In the 12th century Brussels rose to prominence in the province of Brabant, having acquired a certain prosperity as a way-station on the commercial route between the flourishing trade-centres of Bruges and Cologne. Visiting merchants greatly esteemed the town for the skills of its goldsmiths and silversmiths.

By 1235 the city's administration was in the hands of an oligarchy of seven patrician families known as *lignages*. Each contributed an *échevin* or alderman to serve under the prince; the feudal overlord in those days was either the king of France or the emperor of Germany or sometimes even both. Brussels expanded its trade in precious metals with international orders for minting coins. It also started a prosperous textile industry with wool imported from England. Several *béguinages*—nunneries—were set up outside the city and were used by the textile manufacturers as a source of docile and cheap labour at a time when male workers were causing trouble with demands for high wages and better conditions.

The Brussels bourgeoisie was already growing fat and wilful. In 1291 Duke Jean I had to make tax and toll concessions to their municipal treasury. To curtail difficulties with uppity artisans, formation of their guilds was made subject to the approval of the aldermanic oligarchy—a restriction that riled the artisans. Inspired by the example of their **13** brothers in Bruges, who victoriously rose against their French masters at the Battle of the Golden Spurs (*Eperons d'Or*), the Brussels craftsmen led by the weavers and fullers staged a revolt demanding greater representation in city government. Some 36 professional groups were allowed to send a "master of the commune" and "jurors" to participate in administering the town's affairs. Brussels' first experiment in democracy ended three years later when the army of Duke Jean II and the patrician cavalry of the *lignages* defeated the artisans in the bloody battle of Vilvorde (1306), burying alive the ringleaders in ditches outside the city walls.

For the next 50 years the artisans were forbidden to bear arms, and weavers and fullers were not allowed within the city limits after nightfall. But the pressures and uprisings rumbled on until guild privileges were gradually reinstated for such professions as glove- and purse-makers, tailors, carpenters, coopers and cutlers.

Jolly Times Under the Burgundians

Under the dukes of Burgundy, who took control of Brussels at the end of the 14th century,

good times were to be had, if not by one and all, at least by the patrician families and their cronies. When they went into battle, their picnic baskets—as listed in the municipal records —included vast quantities of salmon pâté, trout, eel, all the necessary spices and gallons of local beer and Rhenish wine. In peace time, the *grande bourgeoisie* relaxed in the fashionable steam-baths, *étuves*, where they were tended by pretty girls who served them wine and massaged their aching bones until the first evening bell of the friary announced closing time. Women were allowed in taverns only on Fridays. If caught, they were fined a large sum of money and were obliged, for some unfathomable reason, to relinquish their outer garment. High-living and prudishness went hand in hand as the burghers resisted the establishment of a university in Brussels until 1425, because they feared for the virtue of their daughters at the hands of marauding intellectuals.

The vogue for Brussels cloth declined as English-manufac-

Recycled textile-workers produced Brussels' world-famous tapestries.

tured textiles became too competitive, and it practically disappeared from international markets by 1430. Out-of-work artisans were forced to leave town and the population dropped. But the city compensated for the collapse of the textile industry with the emergence of tapestry weaving. The best of the Brussels weavers were recruited and became much sought after for their skills. Subsequently the French paid the Brussels craftsmen the highest of compliments by attempting to forge their work for foreign markets, even counterfeiting the municipal trademark "B. B." (Bruxella in Brabantia) found at the corner of each authentic Brussels tapestry.

This Burgundian era was a golden age for the arts, van Eyck, van der Weyden, Memling and Bouts being only the best known of a superb school of 15th-century Flemish painters. Civic pride was demonstrated by the great Gothic town halls that sprang up all over Belgium, none surpassing Brussels' own jewel on the Grand-Place, surrounded by the equally grand guildhouses.

The dukes—Philip the Bold, Philip the Good—asserted their supremacy with magnificent pageants and festivities to keep the populace happy. But their dominance began to disintegrate in wars with Louis XI of France. Charles the Bold died at the battle of Nancy in 1477 and his daughter Mary who succeeded him brought the Habsburgs to Brussels by marrying Maximilian of Austria. The city was beset with more troubles—artisans' revolts, famine and plague.

Under the Habsburgs

In 1515, Maximilian's grandson, the future Charles V, made his *entrée solennelle* into Brussels as archduke. He moved into the palace at Coudenberg, the only fixed residence of his peripatetic reign as king of Spain and Holy Roman Emperor. Brussels became the capital of the Low Countries and a great European centre as well. It was here that Charles pronounced his abdication from the Netherlands in 1555.

The great philosopher Erasmus also enjoyed the city's pleasant atmosphere, living for a few months in an elegant house that still stands in Anderlecht. One of his guests was Albrecht Dürer. Also in the 16th century, Pieter Brueghel came to Brussels to paint his marvellous studies of life in the Low Countries. Brussels' flourishing trade in luxury goods was enhanced by the vogue of its lace-makers. Its gunsmiths were equally prized, with Henry VIII of England pleading with Charles V to send a few over to London. But the Brussels city fathers wouldn't let them go.

The Ommegang, perhaps the most spectacular of Brussels' many festivities (still held every year on the first Thursday in July), gave the Renaissance nobility and gentry of Brussels a chance to show off their riches and finery in a dazzling procession around the Grand-Place. Although it began as a religious celebration of a miraculous statue brought to the city in the 14th century, it soon became an unmistakeable assertion of the nobility's civic authority. The high point in the long history of the Ommegang (walk-around) is generally considered to be the day in 1549 when Charles V proudly introduced to the citizens of Brussels his son from Spain, who would become their king, Philip II.

Inquisitions, Beheadings and Bombs

That moment of glorious pageant in fact heralded dark days for the Low Countries' capital. During Charles' reign, the Calvinists arrived in Brussels, and the spiritual rebellion against Catholicism soon became identified with the nationalist rebellion against Spanish rule. Charles issued orders for heretics to be burned, lesser delinquents to be beheaded or drowned and their heads displayed on pikes as a lesson to other recalcitrants. Anyone who denounced a troublemaker would be rewarded with half his property. But Charles only dimly perceived the real threat to Spanish power and never enforced his orders. Son Philip was not so easy-going. He didn't like the Belgians, brought in the Inquisitors, surrounded himself with brutal Spanish soldiers and blood began to flow.

Nationalist resistance was led by William of Nassau, Prince of Orange. Philip, who in 1559 had left Brussels in disgust for Madrid, sent the Duke of Alba—the "bloody Duke"—to quash the revolt. Counts Egmont and Hoorn, more nationalists than rebels, were executed on the Grand-Place in 1568. But the Prince of Orange was able to drive out the Spanish in 1576 and Brussels enacted ferocious **17** anti-Catholic legislation. Religious holidays were banned, Catholic processions forbidden, priests scared to appear in public. In 1581 the Catholic religion itself was quite simply "abolished". That was too much for Philip who sent in a big army under Alexander Farnese and reoccupied Brussels. The Counter-Reformation brought a flood of Jesuits, monks and nuns to Brussels to reinforce the Catholic presence. In the end, the southern provinces of the Low Countries went back to Spain and Catholicism, but the northern provinces (present-day Netherlands) remained largely Protestant and succeeded in breaking away.

Under Philip's daughter Archduchess Isabella and her husband Archduke Albert of

Ommegang pageantry celebrates the grand entry into Brussels of Charles V and son Philip in 1549.

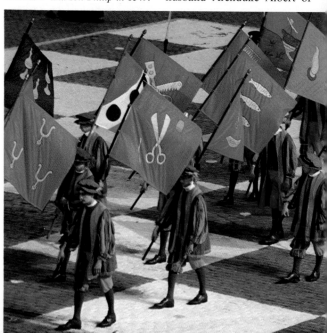

Austria, Brussels returned to some semblance of order (1599–1633). Life in the capital became quite fashionable with the constant flow of ambassadors, generals, bishops and cardinals bringing a new cosmopolitan air to the court of the governors-general around the Sablon quarter. In summer, the chic place to be on a Sunday was the Tivoli Gardens at the royal Domaine de Laeken. The nobility took boat rides on the new Willebroek

Canal which had been built to replace the unreliable River Senne as Brussels' link to the sea, and they went promenading along the Allée Verte. The spirit of the age found artistic expression in the sumptuous and exalted contours of Flemish baroque, which reached its peak in the paintings of Peter Paul Rubens.

At this time, Brussels was a haven for political exiles— Marie de Medici, the dukes of Vendôme and Bouillon, the sons of Charles I of England, Christina of Sweden. But it wasn't quite so safe by the end of the century. In 1695, Louis XIV took revenge for the Dutch and English shelling of his coastal towns with the wanton bombardment of Brussels. Marshal de Villeroi's army of 70,000 men occupied Anderlecht and set up its cannons at the gate of Ninove. For two days, bombs and burning-hot cannonballs battered 4,000 houses, convents and churches. The Grand-Place was particularly badly hit, but the town hall's great bell-tower survived.

The bombs destroyed the Royal Mint and it was replaced by an opera house, the Théâtre de la Monnaie, built by an enterprising Italian banker aptly named Giovanni- **19**

Paolo Bombarda. The city's civic pride quickly found the money and energy to rebuild the rest of the city in its old Renaissance and baroque style, giving the Grand-Place a new architectural harmony that has made it one of the great urban glories of Western Europe.

From One Revolution to Another

The Habsburg Emperor Joseph II ruled Belgium in the last part of the 18th century with a well-meaning but heavy-handed form of enlightened despotism. His religious reforms and judicial liberalization upset the Belgians' profound conservatism and the centralized Vienna-controlled administration upset their ingrown habits of local autonomy, nowhere more than in Brussels. This was at a time when the Americans had thrown off the British yoke and the French were getting rid of their royal one. The old patrician families of Brussels staged a revolt that drove the Austrians out in December 1789 and restored ancient privileges under the Republic of the United States of Belgium. Their reactionary regime was short-lived. The French Revolutionary army arrived in 1792 under General Dumouriez, who supported a more democratic bourgeois government (the Vonckists). The Austrians returned briefly, but the French re-occupied Brussels after the battle of Fleurus in 1794 and this time decided simply to annex Belgium. The French proclaimed the people of Brussels to be *"frères et amis, tous citoyens, tous égaux en droits"* (brothers and friends, all citizens, all equal in rights) with devastating results. Museums and libraries were pillaged, factory equipment requisitioned en masse, all able-bodied men press-ganged into the Revolutionary army.

Napoleon Bonaparte visited Brussels in July 1803. To win over the populace, he had the city's fountains flowing with wine, flattered the leather-craftsmen by ordering their finest luggage, and bought a lace surplice for Pope Pius VII. But, like Louis XIV's bombardment, Napoleon's visit also had important consequences for Brussels' urban development. He laid plans for removing the old ramparts and opening up the avenues and exterior boulevards that give the city its airy aspect today. Another benefit of the "French-ification" was to have the sombre brick façades white-washed to add more light to this northern outpost of Napoleon's empire.

In the winter of 1813–14, Brussels saw the French troops depart, quickly replaced by a procession of Russians, Prussians, Dutch, and finally the English, waiting for orders to go to battle with Napoleon in 1815. The rendezvous was 12 miles away, at Waterloo, on June 17. The day after the battle, Brussels was again full of foreign troops, most of them half-dead.

Napoleon's defeat and the Congress of Vienna led to 16 years of Dutch rule for Belgium, resurrecting the dormant conflicts between Walloons and Flemings. Under Napoleon, French had been Belgium's national language. King William of Orange introduced Dutch, previously spoken only in Flemish communities, into all the schools, municipal governments and law courts. Six hundred families of bureaucrats had to commute between the kingdom's two capitals, The Hague and Brussels, for parliamentary sessions. French-speaking teachers were upset by the imposition of Dutch and taught the

Napoleon is more popular at Waterloo than the victor, Wellington.

POUR L'EM
souvent...
Pour L'EUF
Toujours!

Waterloo:
l'Anxieux Momen

sciences in Latin. The Catholics were upset by the removal of schools from church control. The liberals were upset by press-censorship. Brussels was ready for another revolution.

Independence at Last

In February 1829, a new opera by Daniel François Auber, *La Muette de Portici*, had its première at the Théâtre de la Monnaie. The gala was attended by the Dutch Royal Family, but they did not like what they saw: a rousing story of the Neapolitans' struggles against their oppressors, with an aria *"Amour sacré de la Patrie"* (Sacred love of the fatherland) wildly applauded by the Brussels public. The opera was promptly withdrawn from the repertoire. Its resumption 18 months later was still too soon for Dutch tastes. With Paris overthrowing its monarch in July 1830, revolution was in the air. The Brussels audience on August 25, predominantly young intellectuals of the bourgeoisie, joined in the climactic aria and then left to team up with workers demonstrating on the Place de la Monnaie against their poverty and unemployment. Rioters attacked the Palais de Justice, where liberal journalists were on trial for breaching the censorship laws, and sacked the homes of government ministers while the police and army stood idly by. The next day bakeries were raided for bread, the bars for alcohol, and machinery was smashed in the factories. The bourgeois rebellion for civil rights was threatening to turn into a fully fledged workers' revolt until burgomaster Vanderlinden d'Hooghvorst formed a militia of 8,000 men to quell the riots —and also, reinforced by volunteers from Liège and other provincial cities, to fight the Dutch Army which King William sent to Brussels in September.

Belgium became independent and in July 1831 the keys of the capital were handed over to the new king, Leopold of Saxe-Coburg.

With independence came both phenomenal economic growth and social, political and religious conflicts. Brussels was the arena for constant clashes between a Catholic national government and the liberal municipality, between the Flemings and the Walloons. By resisting universal suffrage, the conservative Catholic provinces maintained control over the government and fueled their fight with the liberals of the capital over schools and church power. Brussels was nominally bilingual, but in fact French increasingly dominated business, the sciences and the state administration. The Flemings campaigned with growing indignation for greater use of their language in the universities and the law courts.

Industrial expansion and imperial adventures in Africa, particularly the Congo, brought great prosperity to Brussels, and the urban planning of Napoleon Bonaparte became a booming reality as splendid mansions and brash commercial buildings sprang up along the new avenues and boulevards. As ever, the luxury industries were at a premium, textiles, lace, furniture, porcelain, paper and printing—the latter benefiting from the flourishing skulduggery of Brussels publishers pirating French best-sellers. (In fact, this industry contributed to popular education by making such authors as Balzac available at cheap prices.)

Brussels was once again a refuge for political exiles—Polish, Italian and French, Russia's Michael Bakunin, Germany's Karl Marx and Friedrich Engels (expelled from Paris in 1845). Marx and Engels organized the socialist German Workers' Club at Le Cygne on the Grand-Place, today a high-class restaurant with very unsocialist prices. They wrote the *Communist Manifesto* in Brussels—and were kicked out of Belgium in 1848 when it was feared they might reproduce the latest Paris revolution.

The national emergence of Belgium in the 19th century also brought an explosion of artistic achievement in the capital. Painters came together in the Groupe des XX in 1883, including Félicien Rops, Fernand Khnopff and James Ensor. Brussels was also a major centre of Art Nouveau architecture under the leadership of Henry van de Velde and Victor Horta.

World Wars and International Leadership

Belgium's historic vulnerability to foreign invasion was hammered home again in August 1914, when Brussels was occupied by Kaiser Wilhelm's German armies. The capital, led by Mayor Adolphe Max, put up a heroic passive resistance to the German occupation. Max was deported to Germany after refusing to provide lists of unemployed who would have been used as forced labour in German factories. One of his wartime successors, Louis Steens, fought German attempts to enlist Flemish collaborators to "de-Frenchify" Brussels. Said Steens after the "Flemification" laws: "I am Flemish and Flemish is my mother tongue, but I don't speak it any more." When the Germans were defeated, Belgium found a new if perhaps short-lived national unity, introducing universal suffrage, the right to strike, a Flemish university and even a truce in the church-schools conflict.

The 1930s saw the emergence in Brussels, as in other European capitals, of fascist groups drawing on social discontent and primitive chauvinism—the Rex, Jeunesses Nationales, Légion Nationale, and a Flemish group, the V.N.V., which appealed to the frustrations of Fleming workers in the capital. The fascist leader Léon Degrelle managed what no other Belgian leader had—he united Catholics, liberals and socialists in a combined effort to defeat him, resoundingly, in the 1937 elections. These grim times offered the natural breeding ground for a flight into the surrealist art of René Magritte and Paul Delvaux and the inspired comic-strip escapism of Hergé's Tintin.

Came World War II and another German occupation, this time finding a few but enough Fascist collaborators to prepare the country for integration into the Thousand Year Reich—principally from among the V.N.V., the Rexists and Heinrich Himmler's favourites, the Flemish fanatics of De Vlag. But while the "Wallonia" and "Flanders" battalions were sending Belgians to die with the German army on the Eastern front, the Légion Nationale joined the underground movement *against* the Germans. Linked to the government-in-exile in London, Belgian resistance was active in organizing the escape of Jews and other endangered residents and in masterminding an elaborate campaign of sophisticated sabotage of the industrial war-machine by Groupe G, engineering graduates from the University of Brussels.

After the war, Belgium was not prepared to take back King Leopold III, who had ordered the army to capitulate in 1940, and he was succeeded in 1951 by his son Baudouin. While Flemings and Walloons continued to squabble, Belgium took on a new role as the internationalist capital of Western Europe and of the At-

King Baudouin and Queen Fabiola have a difficult time keeping the Flemings and the Walloons united.

lantic alliance. In 1957, the European Economic Community made its headquarters in Brussels. The next year the city staged a very successful World's Fair with the optimistic theme: *"Bâtir le monde pour l'homme"* (Building the world for mankind). NATO moved its headquarters to Brussels in 1967 and the city subsequently attracted nearly a quarter of a million permanent foreign residents bustling like bees around the multinational hives of commerce and military organization. Brussel's domestic ethnic balancing act is the perfect microcosm of the problems besetting the international institutions to which it is host, a set of marriages in which the in-laws have to get on together for the sake of the children.

What to See

Brussels starts at the Grand-Place, but you should make your way there by way of the town's world-famous mascot, **Manneken-Pis.** It will put you in the right mood to approach this city, with a sense of humour about the more solemn monuments dear to old-fashioned culture fans. The little boy blithely peeing into a fountain on the Rue de l'Etuve is just 24 inches high, sculpted in bronze in 1619 by Jérôme Duquesnoy. The chubby rascal has become a symbol of Brussels' defiance of an often hostile world; he has been caricatured more than once in the city's satirical magazines as hurrying defeated enemies on their way. Almost as impressive as the statue itself are the myriad versions of him to be found in surrounding souvenir shops—watering cans, ashtrays, bottle-stoppers and even perverse little corkscrews.

Manneken-Pis has an amazingly varied wardrobe of uniforms donated from all over the world and an equally large host of international admirers.

Grand-Place

This is the true centre of town, the liveliest gathering-place, the focus of the city's great historic moments, the most apt expression of its civic pride.

In the 10th century, when the heirs of Charlemagne were making Brussels their citadel, the Grand-Place, at the lower end of the then still visible River Senne, was the town's *Nedermerct* (lower market). Today it still offers a colourful flower-market and on Sunday mornings a marvellously cheerful market for birds. As the surrounding street names still attest—the Rue Chair et Pain, du Poivre, des Harengs, Marché aux Herbes, au Beurre and au Charbon—it was also once the commercial centre for meat, bread, pepper, herrings, spices, butter and charcoal.

In the old days tournaments were held here, with jousts and processions, both religious and profane. Today, on the first Tuesday and Thursday in July, the Ommegang (see p. 86) is still celebrated on the Grand-Place, as descendants of the great patrician families of Brussels don their costumes

---

Finding Your Way

In the bilingual city of Brussels, street and building names appear in both French and Flemish, but for simplicity's sake we've used only the French (spoken by 80 per cent of the population). For the excursions into Flanders where Flemish prevails, we've followed the local practice in citing place-names. Here are some key terms with translations in the two languages to help you along.

	French	*Flemish*
belfry	*beffroi*	*belfort*
bridge	*pont*	*brug*
castle	*château*	*steen, kasteel*
church	*église*	*kerk*
convent	*béguinage*	*begijnhof*
hill	*mont*	*heuvel*
house	*maison*	*huis*
information	*renseignements*	*inlichtingen*
law courts	*palais de justice*	*gerechtshof*
square	*place*	*plein, plaats*
street	*rue*	*straat*

and parade around in the old style, with dances, acrobatics and a climax of human chess played out on a giant checkerboard painted on the paving stones. Even if you're not in town for the Ommegang, you can sit at one of the delightful outdoor cafés and imagine the pageant of bygone days. You may also want to remember that this was the place where celebrities—such as the Count of Egmont in 1568—were beheaded. (Nonentities were done away with on a mound at the site of the present Palais de Justice.)

These days the square is animated by rock concerts and open-air theatre. The Grand-Place has lost none of its festive tone—minus the executions—and remains the best people-watching spot in town. Some of the more snooty residents pretend they never go near the place, claiming it's just for tourists, but in fact you'll find as many natives here as foreign visitors. The red-cheeked faces in the many taverns are right out of Brueghel, very evidently local fauna.

Apart from its lively atmosphere, the Grand-Place is quite simply an architectural masterpiece—for poet Jean Cocteau, "the most beautiful square in the world"; for the rest of us, an undeniable visual joy and well worth a lengthy visit in this town where modern construction has almost effaced the past. Its harmony of Gothic, Renaissance and baroque styles was achieved after the devastating bombardment by Louis XIV's artillery in 1695. The city fathers were forced to plan the restoration with a firm hand, ensuring the unity of its design. The guilds and corporations proudly cooperated in the dignified venture of reconstruction, sparing no expense, as you can see, in the pure gold-leaf façades that glow in the sun.

Louis' cannons, drawn up at the Porte de Ninove, took the soaring tower of the **Hôtel de Ville** (Town Hall) as their principal target, yet, miraculously, that was the one thing that survived. This tower, with its steeple rising 295 feet above the ground, a piece of lace-like stonework, at once massive and graceful, was designed in the 15th century by Jan van Ruysbroeck. At the pinnacle is a statue in gilded copper of the

The Town Hall on the Grand-Place is a Gothic symbol of civic pride.

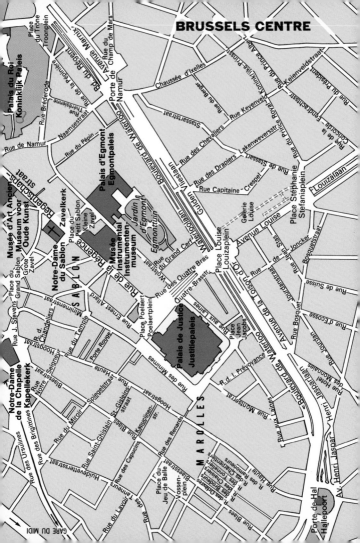

BRUSSELS CENTRE

town's patron saint Michael slaying the devil.

A major part of the Town Hall's charm derives from the off-centre placing of the tower and its entrance. On the right wing, look for three stone carvings on the capitals of the pillars—the "Drinking Monks", the "Estrapade" (a torture in which the victim is dunked in liquid mud) and the "Sleeping Moor" accompanied by his harem. The staircase at the main entrance is flanked by splendid lions and the archway over the door features statues of eight biblical prophets. (The originals of these capitals and prophets are to be found in the municipal museum, see p. 34). Inside the Town Hall, you can visit the Salle du Conseil Communal (Council Room) for its lovely 18th-century tapestries (guided visits only). A Brussels information office, T. I. B., operates in the right wing of the building.

While the Gothic Town Hall may be the dominant feature, the square's elegant human scale is achieved by the magnificent houses of the guilds and corporations which emphasize, better than any dry historical text, the major role played in the city's past by its diligent and prosperous bourgeoisie. Start on the west

side at the corner of the Rue de la Tête d'Or.

The house of the haberdashers (No. 7), known as **Le Renard** (fox), was rebuilt in 1699 in the classical style (which was initiated by the man responsible for the building's destruction four years earlier, Louis XIV). A statue of St. Nicholas, patron of all haberdashers, tops it off. The house of the boatmakers, No. 6, bears their emblem, **Le Cornet** (horn), over the door. The gable below the roof is designed in the shape of a poopdeck of a 17th-century galleon. No. 5, **La Louve** (she-wolf), house of the archers, has a bas-relief above the doorway showing Romulus and Remus being suckled by the wolfmother of Rome. This superb example of High Renaissance style contains four statues on the façade of the second storey representing Truth, Falsehood, Peace and Discord. No. 4, **Le Sac** (bag), house of the cabinet-makers and coopers, has one of the few façades—the first two storeys—that remained intact after the bombardment. No. 3 is named

32

Guild insignia and the bird-market continue the medieval traditions.

La Brouette (wheelbarrow), house of the grease-merchants; Nos. 1 and 2 **Au Roi d'Espagne** (King of Spain), the classical Italian-style house of the bakers, with a charming little statue of Fame atop its octagonal dome.

On the north side of the square, opposite the Town Hall, stands the Maison du Roi (House of the King), which was restored by Charles V but that neither he nor any other king ever lived in. The rebuilt neo-Gothic version of the 19th century is no masterpiece, but its **Musée Communal** Municipal Museum) certainly deserves a visit. On prominent view are some splendid stone sculptures, the 14th- and 15th-century originals of the prophets, monks, torture victim and Moor preserved from the façade of the Town Hall. You'll also see a selection of Brussels tapestries and some excellent 18th-century ceramics from the time when Brussels was a serious rival to Delft. But it's the top floor that draws the biggest crowds, the Manneken-Pis room where the cheeky fellow's incredibly vast wardrobe is displayed—costumes offered by visitors from all over the world, made-to-measure, richly ornamented uniforms of British grenadiers, Japanese samurai, African chiefs and American cowboys.

Next to the Maison du Roi, from Nos. 24 to 28, are **La Chaloupe d'Or** (golden longboat), the house of the tailors; **Le Pigeon,** originally the house of the painters, which, typically, the improverished artists couldn't afford to rebuild after the bombardment; and **La Chambrette de l'Amman,** the house of the Amman, the duke's representative on the town council in the Middle Ages.

On the east side of the square is the impressive Flemish-Italian-style **Maison des Ducs de Brabant** (House of the Dukes of Brabant), named after the statues on the façade's columns rather than the building's owners, who were in fact another group of old corporations.

The first of the three houses that bring us back round to the Town Hall, **L'Arbre d'Or** (golden tree) at No. 10, is the house of the brewers with its columns decorated with ears of wheat and the leaves of hops used in brewing the beer dear to every Belgian's heart and stomach. Inside, you can visit a museum with the replica of an 18th-century brewery, a superb collection of ancient beer-taps and the chance to sample a drop of the good stuff.

Next door is **Le Cygne** (swan) now an elegant restaurant that once appropriately housed the butchers' corporation and then, more piquantly, a tavern where Marx and Engels hatched some of their revolutionary ideas in 1848 and where the Belgian Workers' Party was founded in 1885. And we end up at **L'Etoile** (star), where the Amman stood at the balcony to witness beheadings. In an arcade at the side is a bas-relief of Everard 't Serclaes, a 14th-century alderman shown dying of wounds received in heroic battle against the Count of Flanders. Like thousands before you, rub his arm and the nose of his dog, for good luck.

Around the Grand-Place

The area immediately north of the Grand-Place has been designated **L'Ilot Sacré** (The Sacred Isle). Its name is a veritable cry from the heart of the municipality that finally decided to stand fast against the encroachments of modern property developers who have done more harm to historic Brussels than any foreign bombs or cannonballs. Many of the tiny back streets between the Rue du Marché aux Herbes and the Rue des Bouchers and Rue de l'Ecuyer have been closed to traffic. The old houses have in large part become restaurants, many with restored Renaissance gables, others retaining their coloured-tile, ceramic and stucco façades from the Belle Epoque at the turn of this century. But you'll also find art galleries and craftwork shops there, and in summer the streets are often enlivened with strolling musicians, acrobats, flower-sellers and curiosity vendors.

In the Rue de l'Ecuyer is the entrance to the **Galeries Saint-Hubert,** an attractive complex of glass-vaulted arcades of boutiques and restaurants. It's the Galerie du Roi as far as the Rue des Bouchers, with the Galerie des Princes as a "side-street" and the Galerie de la Reine continuing to the Rue du Marché aux Herbes. The arcades were pioneered in 1846 by Jean-Pierre Cluysenaar and their immediate success among the boomingly prosperous bourgeoisie brought commissions from Milan and Paris. The interlocking galleries have a great **35**

Your walk around the Ilot Sacré will take you over to the **Théâtre de la Monnaie,** the opera house where the first rumbles of the 1830 revolution took place, leading to national independence (see p. 22). North of the neo-classical theatre is the bustling **Place de Brouckère** and the big shopping streets, Boulevard Anspach and Rue Neuve, on the arteries linking the two main railway stations, Gare du Nord and Gare du Midi. All surrounded by bold uncompromising skyscrapers.

It's appropriate to round off this tour with a visit to the ecclesiastical counterpart of the Town Hall, the **Cathédrale Saint-Michel.** Originally dedicated to both St. Michael and St. Gudula, patron and patroness of Brussels' Christian beginnings, this imposing Gothic edifice was elevated to the status of cathedral in 1962. But locals still call it "Saints-Michel et Gudule". The choir dates back to 1226, the nave and transept were added in the 14th and 15th centuries and the chapels built on subsequently. The French-style façade (rarely seen in Belgium) is dominated by two towers of Jan van Ruysbroeck, the twins of his soaring masterpiece on the Town Hall.

advantage in this inner district where so many of the little streets are impasses as a result of property owners in the 19th century and earlier just extending their buildings backwards without reference to any governing town plan—quaint to look at, but tiresomely impractical for merchants.

Ilot Sacré—restaurants in quaint old houses and all-weather shopping in the Galeries Saint-Hubert.

The church suffered destruction at the hands of Calvinists in the 16th century and later on by French revolutionaries, but it has preserved its noble silhouette, rising above the Treurenberg (Mountain of Tears) west of the Rue Royale.

Entering through the south door, the first impression is of the rather sombre choir, but you'll soon see that the transept and nave are suffused with the gentle light of the fine **stained-glass windows.** The five **37**

16th-century windows above the choir portray the city's Spanish, Burgundian and Austrian rulers. The most attractive is undoubtedly the central window showing the Habsburg Archduke Maximilian and his wife Marie of Burgundy with the Virgin Mary.

Hendrik Verbruggen's **pulpit** (1699) is a luxuriant baroque

Intense figures in stained-glass window recreate infamous legend in the Chapelle du St-Sacrement.

affair depicting Adam and Eve fleeing from the Garden of Eden.

The cathedral's artistic masterpiece, the **Chapelle du Saint-Sacrement,** to the left of the choir, was built in 1540 to commemorate a spurious miracle said to have occurred in 1370: Jews were alleged to have stolen the sacraments and stabbed them in ritual defilement on a Good Friday, causing blood to spurt from the sacrament's "wounds". As a

result, four Jewish families in Brussels were burned at the stake.

Against this background, it is difficult but ultimately not impossible to admire the magnificent artistry of the **stained-glass windows** and **tapestries** depicting the story by Bernard von Orley and his pupils.

Underground Art

The Brussels *métro* provides transport—and more. Art has gone underground, transforming tunnels and commuter platforms. All the works on display are by famous Belgian artists. The *Bourse* station features a revolving ceiling sculpture by Pol Bury and a dreamlike painting of tram passengers by the great surrealist Paul Delvaux. At *Comte de Flandre,* 16 soaring bronze figures by Paul Van Hoeydonck, titled *16 × Icarus,* invade the tunnel. The urgent rhythms of Roger Somville's *Notre Temps* pulsate just above the tracks at *Hankar,* while ceramic tile designs by Jo Delahaut and Jean-Michel Folon's *Magic City* decorate *Montgomery* station.

The Société des Transports Intercommunaux de Bruxelles publishes a brochure describing the art in the *métro,* with several suggested itineraries to follow.

Le Sablon

When you want to retreat from 20th-century Brussels back to a more peaceful time, head for the Sablon area, south of the Grand-Place. Now perhaps the most elegant district of pre-19th-century Brussels, the Sablon (in French, a sandy wasteland) was originally inhabited only by a hermit—with its marshes providing a burial ground for the overflow from the St-Jean hospital. These grim beginnings were soon forgotten when the guild of the crossbowmen built the chapel of Notre-Dame in 1304. And the Sablon's glory was assured by the transfer of a miraculous healing Virgin Mary statue from Antwerp, making the church a great attraction for pilgrims.

The **Place du Grand Sablon** is graced by antique shops, charming restaurants in handsomely restored 17th- and 18th-century houses and a weekend antique market. The square forms a harmonious ensemble with the north side of the church.

On the south side, the **Square du Petit Sablon** offers a peaceful Renaissance-style garden peopled with 19th-century bronze statues. Foremost

Notre Dame du Sablon is a fine Gothic church in an old quarter of town popular with antique dealers.

among them—the great martyrs of Belgium, Counts Egmont and Hoorn. The Egmonts were one of the many aristocratic families who made the Sablon their home in the 16th century. It was the centre of a fashionable cosmopolitan capital when the Austro-Spanish court enjoyed its heyday under Archduke Albert and Archduchess Isabella. The restored and renovated **Palais d'Egmont** at the southern end of the square has been surrounded by many political controversies during its long history, not the least of them being the one unleashed by the signature there of Britain's entry into the European Common Market.

The church of **Notre-Dame du Sablon,** a masterpiece of Belgian Gothic, took on its present shape in the early 15th century. As you enter the church on the south side, take a look at the elegant porch crowned by fine rose-shaped stonework. The interior boasts a marvellous 17th-century baroque **pulpit,** an exuberant outburst of angels, cherubim and saints carved by Marcus

de Vos. The pulpit proper is supported by a vigorous sculpture of the evangelical symbols of Matthew, Mark, Luke and John. The choir has a fine sweep to it, and on its left the sacrarium contains a notable *Adoration of the Magi.* Next to that is the chapel of the family of Thurn and Taxis, nobles who started the first European postal service in the early 16th century with headquarters at their house in the Sablon. The chapel, which houses the family's sepulchres, is built in stark black marble with the white statuary and ornamentation of Lucas Faydherbe in dramatic contrast.

Knocking off the Bird

Notre-Dame du Sablon was historically as much a focus of festivity as a place of worship. In 1530 Margarete of Austria organized a procession there to celebrate delivery from a plague and the festivities quickly turned into Brussels' annual July funfair. In 1615 the Archduchess Isabella delighted the crossbowmen by shooting down the bird-emblem of their *Grand Serment* (Great Oath) from the steeple of the church. The crack markswoman was carried shoulder high through the streets and Brussels took off the next three days to celebrate.

Les Marolles

Moving slightly to the west, the city's other Gothic church of note is the **Notre-Dame de la Chapelle** at the fork of the Rue Haute and Rue Blaes on the north end of the popular quarter known as the Marolles. This is the most appropriate last resting place of the great populist painter, Pieter Brueghel, who died in 1569. His marble mausoleum is marked by a sad story all too illustrative of the human frailty he loved to depict. At the request of Brueghel's son, Rubens painted a picture in tribute to the great master, *Christ Handing the Keys to St. Peter,* but the church sold the painting in 1765 and it now has only a copy.

In all probability—but the experts are not 100 per cent sure—Pieter Brueghel lived and died just down the street from the church, at 132, rue Haute. At any rate, it's a fine old gabled **house** faithfully restored in the beamed style of the period (1563–69), a house that the master might well have inhabited. Above all, the neighbourhood itself, the Marolles around the Rue Haute and Rue Blaes is a delight for the busy street life in this old working-class district where

Brussels historically kept its sense of humour whenever the rest of the town was falling apart. Linguists will appreciate the rich dialect mixing Flemish, French, Spanish and smatterings of Italian, German and Hebrew—a veritable inventory of the invaders and refugees who have passed through over the centuries.

The names of the streets bunched between the Rue Blaes and Rue Haute bear witness to the fact that this is

above all a working neighbourhood—Rue des Orfèvres (goldsmiths), des Brodeurs (emboiderers), des Chaisiers (chair-makers), des Tonneliers (coopers), des Charpentiers (carpenters) and des Ramoneurs (chimney-sweeps). Their corporations gathered around the Grand-Place; this is where the work was done.

At the southern end of the Marolles, take a look at the **Porte de Hal,** last vestige of the city's medieval fortified ramparts. It's a grand horseshoe-shaped gate built in the 14th century, after the Count of Flanders had been driven out, built to stop anyone like him from coming back. The façade facing the city-centre is a 19th-century addition, but the rest is the original masonry.

Neighbourhood of Les Marolles is brightened up by street murals.

Coming back towards the centre, it's difficult to miss the gigantic **Palais de Justice,** the biggest building erected in the 19th century. Altogether, it covers 6.5 acres, including the spot where they used to hang common criminals (the uncommon ones being kept for the Grand-Place). The years of its construction—1866–83—spanned the period of Belgium's spectacular economic, industrial and even imperial growth, and the sprawling, soaring neo-Greco-Roman structure is the bombastic epitome of its age. You have to be impressed—if only by the sheer gall of the thing. To build the Palais de Justice, it was necessary to raze a large part of the Marolles and to this day the world "architect" has a definitely pejorative sense in the district.

The Rue de la Régence leads from the Palais de Justice to the Place Royale and the **Palais du Roi,** official town residence of the king of Belgium. Built in the 18th century on the site of the old court of Brussels, it is generally open to the public for a period in late summer.

All over town you catch a glimpse
44 *of the gigantic Palais de Justice.*

Museums

And now for the main attractions of the Place Royale: the **Musées Royaux des Beaux Arts,** where the creative genius of the Low Countries is shown to splendid advantage. The museums are divided into the Musée d'Art Ancien (art up to the mid-19th century) and the Musée d'Art Moderne (late 19th and 20th centuries), with the Bibliothèque Royale (Royal Library) between them.

The **Musée d'Art Ancien** was founded in 1799 as a depository for whatever the French revolutionary armies couldn't carry back to Paris. After Waterloo, the greater part of the plunder was recuperated, constituting now a collection of some 1,200 paintings, most of them from the great Flemish schools. Pride of place goes to Brueghel and Rubens, but it is worth lingering over some of the other masters of the Low Countries, both wistful and exuberant in tone, subtle and robust in style.

Start with the Master of Flémalle, probably Robert Campin, early 15th-century teacher of the more celebrated Roger van der Weyden. His *Annunciation* shows the angel revealing to Mary her divine destiny in the charming setting of a Flemish bourgeois home.

Most of the best work of **Roger van der Weyden** (c. 1399–1464), Brussels' official municipal painter, was destroyed by Louis XIV's bombardment in 1695. But his sorrowful *Pietà* and expressive *Man with an Arrow* are excellent examples of his style.

One of the jewels of the Brussels collection is *The Judgement of Emperor Otto* by **Dirk Bouts** (c. 1415–75). The diptych relates the episode in which Otto was duped by his wife into beheading an innocent man *(Punishment of the Innocent)* and then recognizes his error when the widow faces the *Ordeal by Fire*. Only the consummate control of a Dutch painter could capture these horrible events with such cool beauty and reserve.

You'll notice something of the same detachment in *The Martyrdom of St. Sebastian* by **Hans Memling** (c. 1435–94), where the precise skills of the archers are given as much emphasis as the almost imperceptible suffering of Sebastian.

Because many paintings by **Hieronymus Bosch** (c. 1450–1516) seem full of menace, monsters and weird surrealism, the more conventional *Crucifixion* here may come as

Brueghel's Fall of Icarus typifies the master's cynical cheerfulness.

a surprise. All the same, Bosch just couldn't resist throwing in the nasty little black raven of death on the left above a skull and a few bones of previous crucifixion victims.

Pieter Brueghel (c. 1525–69) is splendidly represented. *The Fall of Icarus* is a marvellous epitome of the master's mixture of serenity and cynicism, showing peasants going about their work while poor Icarus falls into the sea, a literal illustration of the old Flemish proverb that "no plough stops for a dying man". Brueghel's acute social observation in *The Census at Bethlehem* transposes the census taking in the Palestine desert to tax collection in the snows of Flanders. Another winter landscape, *Skaters and Bird Trap*, threatens the picture's fragile tranquillity with the distinct

impression that the skaters might at any moment fall through the holes in the ice and the birds topple the trap that is over their heads.

Peter Paul Rubens (1577–1640) is displayed in strength. You should look especially for his unusual studies of *Negro Heads,* and you'll find the smiling face reproduced in one of the three Magi in *The Adoration of the Magi.* Two more characteristically exuberant Rubenesque Rubens are

The Way of the Cross, which makes the climb to Calvary more triumphant than tragic, and the ferocious *Martyrdom of St. Livinius,* in which a magnificent scarlet-hatted bandit has torn out the poor bishop's tongue with a pair of pincers.

Calm down a bit with the restfully domestic *Portrait of a Genoese Lady and her Daughter* by **Anthony van Dyck** (1599–1641) and **Frans Hals'** (1580–1666) *Group of Children,* as smug a bunch of kids as you could wish to find anywhere.

The German painter **Lucas Cranach** (1472–1553) is represented by a rather naughty-looking *Eve* and a still innocent *Adam.* His portrait of *Dr. Scheyring* is a masterpiece of no-nonsense civic dignity.

Rembrandt (1606–69) gets rather short shrift in Brussels, but his cool, distinguished portrait of *Nicolaas van Bambeeck* deserves your attention.

To give you some idea of what the Spanish were like when they ruled Brussels, take a look at *Apollo Flaying Marsyas* by José de Ribera (c. 1591–1652). Having discarded his lyre, Apollo is calmly skinning Marsyas alive. Look, too, for another famous death scene: David's *Marat Assassinated in his Bathtub.* **47**

and Paul Delvaux, each taking a pot-shot at the bourgeoisie from a variously erotic, satiric, or surreal point of view. Foreign moderns run the gamut from Matisse to Henry Moore. You can't miss Saul Steinberg's witty mural of America, on show in the entrance hall.

Among the city's other museums, you should not fail to visit the **Musées Royaux d'Art et d'Histoire** in the south-east corner of the Parc du Cinquantenaire. You'll find a whole panorama of world civilization. The vast collections range from the ancient arts of Mesopotamia, Egypt, Iran, Greece and Rome to Oriental masterpieces of Cambodia, China, Korea, Japan and India; pre-Columbian sculpture of the Mayans and Aztecs from Mexico and Peru; Brussels and Tournai tapestries, Delft china and Brussels lace; plus a superb collection of 18th-century carriages, coaches, sedan-chairs, sleighs and horse-drawn trams on view in the Musée de la Voiture.

Music-lovers will appreciate the **Musée Instrumental** on the Rue de la Régence near the Square du Petit-Sablon (in the Conservatoire). The substantial collection includes rare European instruments from

Musées Royaux d'Art et d'Histoire, Bruxelles

Later art favours the French —Delacroix, Courbet and Sisley.

A passageway takes you to the refurbished, subterranean **Musée d'Art Moderne,** also accessible via Place Royale. Among the Belgian masters on display are Rik Wouters, **48** James Ensor, René Magritte the 16th to 18th centuries, as well as some fascinating instruments from China, Sumatra, Java, Iraq and Mexico.

Those with a taste for the graceful style of Art Nouveau, which the Belgians did much to pioneer at the turn of the century, should visit the **Musée Horta** (25, rue Américaine, off the Chaussée de Charle-roi), installed in the house built by Victor Horta in 1898. The windows, mirrors, staircase, woodwork and wrought iron of the house itself show how Art Nouveau brought a new decorative dimension to the most utilitarian objects. The museum includes superb pieces of furniture and artefacts salvaged from houses such as the 1896 Maison du Peuple, demolished by the city's voracious property developers.

Belgian art favours children—from medieval statues to modern Tintin.

Peripheral Attractions

One of the few **Art Nouveau houses** still standing in Brussels—but luckily also one of the most beautiful—can be seen at 224, **avenue Louise,** the city's most elegant shopping street. In case you begin to think that Brussels' bourgeoisie is nothing but a bunch of tasteless philistines, it's worth wandering around the gracious residential neighbourhoods on and around the **Squares Marie-Louise** and **Ambiorix** in the St. Josse district, the **Jardin du Roi** in Ixelles or the **Avenue Winston Churchill** in the district of Le Chat. The good life here is very much in evidence, an impression to be reinforced if you drive around the spacious exterior Boulevards du Souverain and de la Woluwe.

Following Avenue Louise south, you pass by the old restored Cistercian **Abbaye de la Cambre** in Ixelles. The cloister, rebuilt in the 1930s, is made to order for your quiet meditations. The statuary, stained-glass and paintings inside the 14th-century church are mostly modern in origin, but there is a fine head of Christ by the 15th-century artist, Albert Bouts.

One of the illustrious men of the Renaissance, the great humanist Erasmus, lived for a short time in Brussels. The **House of Erasmus,** in the borough of Anderlecht (Rue du Chapitre), has been turned into an attractive museum of the philosopher's career, with paintings, original manuscripts and letters exchanged with the

great men of his times. But you can also enjoy the visit for the charm and tranquillity of the house itself. The lovely Gothic structure has Renaissance additions around the courtyard, a harmonious ensemble of Spanish and Netherlands styles. While in Anderlecht, take a look at the **Béguinage** (at the end of the Rue du Chapelain), a 16th-century

Old lampposts light the way as night falls beside the Parc de Bruxelles.

nunnery where eight nuns lived and worked at the budding lace industry.

You might be interested in visiting the Parc des Expositions where Brussels held its World Fair in 1958, if only for the view of the city from the top (reachable by lift) of the **Atomium,** a magnification by 200,000 million times of an iron crystal molecule. In the top atom, made of aluminium-covered steel, is a luxury restaurant and in the bottom atom an exhibition on space exploration and the peaceful uses of nuclear energy.

... and Parks

Brussels is also a city of magnificent parks. One of them lies in the very heart of the city, the **Parc de Bruxelles,** off the Rue Royale between the Palais du Roi and Palais de la Nation. It has a special place in the capital's history for it was there that the Dutch army was hemmed in by the Belgian revolutionary militia in the victorious fight for independence during the "glorious days" of September 1830. Today the fountains and children play among graceful baroque and rococo statues.

Just east of the Rond Point Schuman, where the Euro-pean Community has its headquarters, is the **Parc du Cinquantenaire.** It was laid out in 1880 to celebrate Belgium's 50th anniversary of independence and is the home of three museums: the Musées Royaux d'Art et d'Histoire (see p. 48); the Musée Royal de l'Armée et d'Histoire Militaire, an immense collection of weapons, uniforms, models of workshops and aircraft; and **Autoworld,** one of the world's biggest collections of vintage cars. Continuing along the Avenue de Ter-vuren, you reach the **Parc de Woluwe,** bordering on the "beaux quartiers" of the south-east.

Lovers of botanical gardens flock out every spring to the park at the **Domaine Royal de Laeken** (No. 357 bus), preferred playground of the Spanish and Austrian nobility in the 16th and 17th centuries. At the top end of the Avenue du Parc Royal you will find the royal greenhouses *(Serres Royales)*, beautifully illuminated at night during the month of May. Nearby are a Japanese tower and Chinese pavilion.

But the citizens' favourite park remains the **Bois de la Cambre** at the far end of the Avenue Louise, a 15-minute tram or bus ride. Known simply as the "Bois", amid groves of superb beech trees and boating lakes, restaurants and tea-rooms, it's the perfect place to rest your aching feet while the kids run and roller-skate.

The Bois de la Cambre is in fact only the municipal tip of the gigantic **Forêt de Soignes** which extends over to the **Parc de Tervuren** to form a wonderful massive curtain of dense green forest and rolling parkland across the south-east corner of Brussels. This was where Charles V and his aunt Margarete of Austria and sister Maria of Hungary loved to go hunting, in an area that is today the site of the gardens of Le Logis and Floréal. There is a superb Arboretum at Tervuren and the forest has splendid lakes for boating and watersports, one of the most popular being the Lac de Genval. Or,

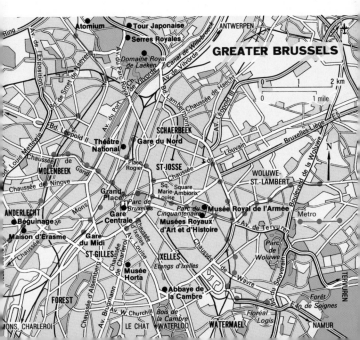

for a change of pace, visit the **Musée Royal de l'Afrique Centrale** for its fine collection on African art, ethnology and natural history. At the far end of the forest is the **Château de Rixensart,** a graceful, red-brick Renaissance structure belonging to the Princes de Merode. There is a fine cloister-like

Brussels is surrounded by plenty of spacious parks and the Bois de la Cambre is splendid for boating.

courtyard and the interior is richly furnished in Louis XV and Louis XVI style with tapestries from Beauvais and Gobelins.

Excursions

All the points suggested here can be reached in a couple of hours by road or rail from Brussels. Waterloo is closest, a 20-kilometre drive south on the N5 or a short train (Brussels-Charleroi line) or bus ride away. For the other destinations, a logical itinerary would be to start off with Antwerp (46 km. to the north), then head west (59 km.) to take in Ghent and (49 km.) Bruges, from which it's just a short hop (27 km.) to Ostend and other resorts on the coast. Any one of these places can be seen on a day's outing from Brussels, or they could be combined with a more extensive tour of Flanders.

Waterloo

History buffs, of course, will need no encouragement to make this trip out of Brussels. In fact, few people with the curiosity to come to Belgium in the first place will want to miss this landmark in European history, the site of the battle that ended Napoleon's Empire. There is something extraordinarily moving about standing amid the peaceful farmlands south of the Belgian capital and imagining the turmoil, tumult and bloodshed in that pelting rain and mud of June 18, 1815. The fighting of just half a day left some 50,000 dead and wounded among the 188,000 French, British, Prussian, Dutch and Belgian soldiers who saw action at Waterloo.

The town of Waterloo itself, 5 kilometres north of the battlefield, has a **Wellington Museum** in the house where the British general set up his headquarters on the eve of battle. The museum includes maps, battle plans and letters and the original furniture in Wellington's bedroom.

South of the battlefield, at Vieux-Genappe, is the **Ferme du Caillou,** the farm where Napoleon had his headquarters, also transformed into a museum, with the great little man's camp bed, hat and utensils.

At the **Butte du Lion** (easily visible west of the N5) is a monument built by the Dutch to honour the Prince of Orange on the spot where he was wounded. The mound (with a cast-iron lion that is not, contrary to legend, cast from melted-down cannons and cannonballs) gives a fine overall view of the battlefield. **55**

Climb the mound to see the various positions taken across the plain by the opposing armies. But everything from up there looks deceptively flat. You can't begin to appreciate the hazards and advantages of each military formation until you walk around the battlefield itself, seeing it from the poor soldier's point of view. Every dip, hollow and slightest rise in the ground made a difference of life and death.

At the base of the mound is a museum with a painted panorama of the battlefield and audiovisual account of the fighting. In the inevitable souvenir shop, you may be amused to see that busts of the loser Napoleon outnumber those of the winners Welling-

Now quiet, La Haie-Sainte farm saw some fierce fighting at Waterloo's great battle.

ton and Blücher about 500 to 1.

Arm yourself with an illustrated guide to the battlefield and a pair of binoculars to appreciate the strategic importance of such redoubts as the farms of Hougoumont, La Haie-Sainte and Papelotte where the fiercest pitched battles took place. Try to visit at least **Hougoumont,** south-west of the Butte du Lion, where the walls of the farmyard carry a modest plaque of the British Coldstream Guards, who helped liberate Belgium in 1944, in honour of their fallen comrades of Waterloo. The bullet scars of 1815 still pockmark the masonry.

Standing at the northern end of the battlefield, at Wellington's position above **La Haie-Sainte,** you can appreciate his enormous advantage, with infantry concealed behind a crest at his back, looking down on the exposed French armies around La Belle-Alliance less than a mile to the south. But Napoleon's soldiers were better disciplined and experienced and the battle was very close until Blücher's Prussian troops arrived from Wavre to tip the balance. **La Belle-Alliance,** the farm where Blücher and Wellington met to congratulate each other after the battle, still stands.

Antwerp
Pop. 750,000

Though it never held the status of a capital in the political life of the Low Countries, the economic and cultural prominence of Antwerp *(Antwerpen/ Anvers)* made it for a long period perhaps the most important town in northern Europe, the north pole of a trading and artistic axis that included Florence, Genoa and Venice. The peak of its power came in the 15th century, when Bruges' access to the sea silted up and Antwerp's River Schelde was widened by flooding. Thereafter, Antwerp became the principal port of the Low Countries. Its dominant position continued well into the 16th century as a clearinghouse for all the new riches—spices, silks, gold and precious stones—brought back by the Portuguese from the Indies. This was the town to which Peter Paul Rubens was proud to return and make his home during the most glorious years of his life, the town where Christophe Plantin created Europe's greatest printing plant.

Today, nurtured by tough Flemish diligence, the port is booming again, rivalling Rotterdam and Hamburg as a gateway for Europe's imports **57** and exports. Antwerp also shares with Amsterdam the monopoly on diamond cutting for the world market. The town's prosperity has enabled it, despite the devastations of World War II, to preserve and restore the great monuments of its past—a magnificent cathedral, a *grand-place* to match that of the capital, Rubens' splendid residence and rich collections of art in its museums. These, together with the animation of its port life, make Antwerp a delightful one-day excursion, with the calculated risk that you might end up staying longer.

Approach the great cathedral across the triangular **Handschoenmarkt** (glove market) with its ornate well attributed to Quentin Massys, a leading Flemish portrait painter. The statue above is of the town's legendary hero Silvius Brabo.

The **Kathedraal** *(Onze Lieve Vrouw)*, undergoing extensive restoration to recover the original creamy white tones of its masonry, is a wonderful 14th- and 15th-century Gothic edifice. Like many other churches of that era, it resembles a mother hen with an assortment of houses built right onto its walls. Though architectural purists sometimes com-

plain that they conceal important elements of the cathedral's exterior design, this is more than compensated for by the powerful impression of a church inexorably integrated into its parish.

But the beauty of the cathedral derives above all from the majesty purity of its open stonework **steeple**, 400 feet high, rising over the octagonal dome at the other end of the church. The spacious interior also conveys the essential

nobility of the church, a feeling that is reinforced by the **Rubens masterpieces** that decorate it. His works include a triptych in the right transept showing the descent of Christ's body from the cross; the altarpiece in the choir, a glowing *Assumption;* and the titanic *Raising of the Cross* in the left transept, painted in 1610 just after Rubens had returned from Italy full of Rome's Renaissance splendour.

Of the church's ten chapels, the largest is St. Anthony's, notable for the fine 1503 stained-glass window showing Henry VII of England kneeling with his queen. The window commemorated, appropriately enough for mercantile

Antwerp's historic role as a trading and artistic centre rivalling Florence and Venice and its vitality today derive from its important and lively port.

Antwerp, a commercial treaty between England and the Low Countries.

South of the cathedral is **Groenplaats** (Green Square) which was once the church cemetery and is now a lively square with open-air cafés bordering a tree-shaded centre with a statue of Rubens.

As in Brussels, Antwerp's **Grote Markt** (or Grand-Place) emphasizes the primordial role that the burghers of the self-assertive corporations played in its history. The **Stadhuis** (Town Hall) is a shining monument of municipal pride, a towering structure that embodies Antwerp's historic position linking northern and southern Europe, combining Italian Renaissance columns with the Gothic lattice-windows and gables typical of the Low Countries. Among the **corporations' houses,** the most impressive are No. 3, De Witte Engel (House of the White Angel); No. 5, Het Kuiperhuis (House of the Coopers); No. 7, finest of them all, De Oude Voetboog (House of the Old Crossbow); and No. 11, Meerseniershuis (House of the Haberdashers). All have been

Statue of the city's hero, Silvius Brabo, with the evil giant's hand.

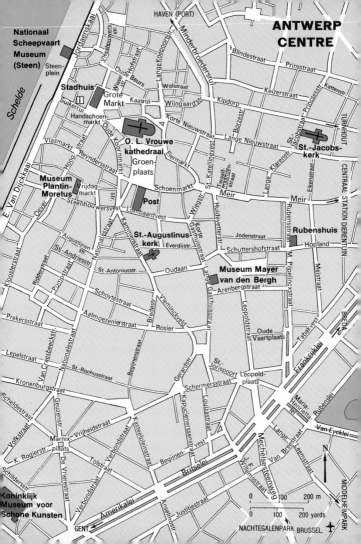

faithfully restored in their 16th-century Flemish Renaissance style. The 19th-century Brabo fountain on Grote Markt is by Jef Lambeaux. Silvius Brabo is said to have chopped off an evil giant's hand and thrown it away, thus making the town safe from tyranny and providing it with a name—*hand werpen* (handthrow).

Rubenshuis (Rubensstraat 9–11, off the main street of the Meir) offers lavish proof that Rubens hardly fit the conventional view of a famous but impoverished artist. He made a lot of money painting for the greatest monarchs of Europe and built himself a sumptuous house in 1610 when he came to Antwerp to spend the last 30 years of his life.

As a residence for his family of eight children by two wives, Isabella Brant and Hélène Fourment, the left wing of the house was, in traditional Flemish style, rather austerely furnished, but the tastes Rubens acquired in Italy were given free rein when it came to equipping his studio in the right wing. This opulently baroque side of the house also served as a museum for his vast personal collection of ancient Greek and Roman sculpture and Flemish and Italian

paintings, much of which is on display today. The collection includes paintings by Jordaens, Snyders, Jan Brueghel and Veronese, plus of course several of his own paintings, with a self-portrait in the dining-room.

The late-Gothic church **Sint Jacobskerk** (east of the cathedral) is worth a visit for the splendid art on view inside, especially the **Rubens Chapel** behind the choir where the artist and his family are buried. The painting over the altar is one of the master's last works, in which, according to experts, he has depicted his two wives as the Madonna and Mary Magdalen and himself as Saint George.

One of the most fascinating windows on Antwerp's golden age of the 16th century is the **Plantin-Moretus Museum** (Vrijdagmarkt 22). It's the elegant Renaissance house of Christophe Plantin, one of the most important craftsmenbusinessmen of the Spanish empire's heyday. Plantin's house and the printing presses housed next door present a marvellous history of printing, books and of the evolution of handwriting itself. Seven of the printing presses—there were 16 at one time—have been kept in perfect working order

One of the master's lusty men seems to be puzzled about just what it is that makes a Rubenesque woman—La Femme au Perroquet—so desirable.

and the museum will run off a copy of a sonnet by Plantin as a souvenir. But the most precious exhibit of the collection is the revered **Biblia Regia** or Polyglot Bible, printed in 1568–72 in eight volumes, in Hebrew, Syriac, Aramaic, Latin and Greek. The foreign collection includes one of the best surviving Gutenberg Bibles, from 1455, and a very rare copy of the Papal Index of forbidden books, from 1569. Rubens has obliged with some fine family portraits.

The **Koninklijk Museum voor Schone Kunsten** (on the Volkstraat south of the cathedral) has a first-class collection of Flemish art in a tastefully modernized setting. Pride of place is, of course, once again given to Rubens, with magnificent versions of *Adoration of the Magi* and *St. Francis of Assisi,* but his followers Jordaens and van Dyck are also admirably represented. Among the earlier works to look out for: an altar triptych by Roger van der Weyden depicting the **63**

Seven Sacraments; a portrait of Jean de Candida by Hans Memling; *The Honest Judges* and *The Holy Women* by Dirk Bouts; and two exquisite works by another Antwerp master, Quentin Massys, *Mary Magdalen* and *The Burial of Christ.* In the modern collection you can admire Belgium's particular contribution to the surreal vision of our times, prefigured by James Ensor at the turn of the century and brought to fruition by René Magritte and Paul Delvaux in the 1930s. Foreign artists include Modigliani, Lovis Corinth, Rodin and Zadkine.

If Brussels whetted your appetite for Pieter Brueghel, visit the **Mayer van den Bergh Museum** (at the corner of Lange Gasthuisstraat and Arenbergstraat). There you can see his vehemently pessimistic vision of war, *Dulle Griet* (Angry Maggie), and the *Twelve Proverbs,* his earliest known signed work. Other highlights include a lovely *Virgin and Child* by van der Weyden and a *Crucifixion* triptych by Quentin Massys.

Antwerp possesses one of Europe's most important **Zoological Gardens** (*Dierentuin,* behind the Central Railway Station). Every effort is made to give the animals as much freedom and normal environment as possible. The collection of gorillas and orang-outangs is outstanding. But the zoo's most striking feature is the innovative system of bird cages-without-cages. The exotic birds are able to fly freely among trees and foliage without coming into contact with the public—or escaping—by an ingenious system of lighting that keeps the birds illuminated and the spectators in darkness.

If this puts you in the mood for trees and greenery, go south to **Nachtegalen** and **Middelheim parks,** the latter with a delightful open-air sculpture museum that includes pieces by Rodin, Henry Moore and Maillol.

Before visiting the port, a must if you want to appreciate the historic and modern personality of Antwerp, stop off at the **Nationaal Scheepvaart Museum** (Maritime Museum). It's housed in a 16th-century castle known as the **Steen** on the right bank of the River Schelde. The museum will give you a keen sense of the importance of the sea in Antwerp's long history, with collections ranging from intricate maritime maps, ancient nautical instruments and seafaring paraphernalia, to the weird mysticism surrounding the mythic figureheads that adorned the prows of ships plying the seas to make Antwerp's fortune. Children especially will love the meticulous boat models and fiendishly clever boats-in-a-bottle.

Properly primed for the sea, you can take a tour around the great **port** *(haven)* of Antwerp. The best way to see it is on one of the regular boat trips that leave from the Steen and last 50 minutes or three hours, depending on the degree of your passion for shipping. Try to go on a weekday when port activity is at its greatest along the 50 miles of quays and docks. As you move among the little cargo-boats and monster oil tankers, you'll be able to get a close look at the work of loading and unloading the huge containers on the ships, repairing and refitting in any one of 18 dry-docks, as well as the operations of the six gigantic sluices linking the river with the docks. Antwerp claims that its port is "the fastest in the world" at getting a ship in, unloading, reloading and getting it out to sea again. Your tour will show you all the sounds, movements and sometimes pungent smells of this vital enterprise in Belgium's economy.

Ghent
Pop. 250,000

Ghent (*Gent* in Flemish, *Gand* in French) is the very epitome of the fiercely independent-minded Flemish municipality. The town first made its mark in history in A.D. 610, when its pagan inhabitants threw the Christian missionary St. Amand into the River Schelde. And though it was the birthplace of the great Charles V, the residents were not about to accept the taxes he tried to impose without a fight. The people of Ghent have never liked to be taken for granted. They made their fortune in wool, sided with their suppliers, the English, against the French and then, at the beginning of the 19th century, were happy to let the French reorganize their textile industry. Today, an ambitious restoration programme is busy sustaining the Gothic and Renaissance splendours of Ghent's past while coping with the rigorous demands of the 20th-century industry and urban expansion.

When you reach the town, make straight for the middle of the **Sint-Michielsbrug** (St. Michael's Bridge). From this vantage point you can look around 360 degrees over one of the most delightful urban **65** vistas in the world. To the east, you see the three towers of St. Bavon's Cathedral, the belfry and the Church of St. Nicholas; to the south, the apse of the Church of St. Michael and its reflection in the River Lieve; to the north the ominous crenellated ramparts and turrets of the Gravensteen, castle of the counts of Flanders; and then immediately below you, the magnificently weathered façades of the old Flemish Gothic and Renaissance merchants' houses of the Graslei (Grass Quay) on the right and Koornlei (Corn Quay) on the left.

The architectural glory of Ghent, on a very human, easily accessible scale, is the **Graslei,** whose houses are a marvel of subtle colour, graceful form and ornamental detail. As you look from the bridge, from right to left, you can see the **House of the Free Bargemen.** Its gently curving roof built in 1531 modifies the traditional right-angled crow-steps of Flemish-Gothic, giving an almost baroque flavour to the upper storey. Next to that are the red-brick **House of the Grain Measurers** (1698), the smaller **Toll-House,** where a fee in grain was paid for right of passage on the river, and then, in stark contrast to the

surrounding buildings, the oldest, an austere but attractive Romanesque **Warehouse** of 1200. Of the houses on the other bank, the **Koornlei,** the most appealing is the **House of the "Unfree" Bargemen** (who didn't enjoy the privileges of Free Bargemen) at No. 7, a late-baroque house of 1740.

Walk back from St. Michael's Bridge to the imposing 15th-century **Lakenhalle** (Drapers' Hall), centre of Ghent's ancient prosperity. In the huge Gothic assembly hall, against a model of the town in the 16th century, you can see a multilingual "sound-and-light" show entitled "Ghent and Charles V". It recounts the story of the city's steadfast refusal to pay taxes to finance the wars of the emperor, despite the fact that he was born in Ghent.

Ghent's genteel houses seen from the ramparts of the Gravensteen.

Soaring above the Laken-halle is the great 300-foot **bel-fry** *(Belfort)*, symbol since 1321 of the town's civic freedoms, a constant visual challenge to the cathedral, whose spiritual power was more often allied with that of the reigning monarch, duke or emperor.

The **Town Hall** *(Stadhuis)* is a strange but not unattractive mixture made up of the late-Gothic Charter House facing on Hoogpoort and a Renaissance wing facing Botermarkt to the east. The Gothic façade is as decorative as a flamboyant cathedral, with a splendid balcony for proclamations, while the Renaissance façade is more stately, almost solemn, with elegant lattice windows flanking the staircase to its high-columned doorway.

Sint-Baafskathedraal (St. Bavon's Cathedral) is certainly one of the finest Gothic churches of the Low Countries, a harmonious subtly hued structure of buttermilk and grey stone and red-brick. Construction began in the 13th century (the choir) and was completed in the 16th with the tower (which lost its steeple in a fire in 1603).

The Church princes in van Eyck's The Adoration of the Mystic Lamb.

The Itinerant Lamb

The van Eyck masterpiece has not had an easy life. The people of Ghent had to protect it from the thieving hands of Philip II and the iconoclastic flames of the Protestants. Emperor Joseph II, who prided himself on being an enlightened liberal, was embarrassed by the nudity of Adam and Eve on the painting's side-panels, and they were replaced with clothed versions—theologically dubious because Eve hadn't eaten her apple yet. The French revolutionaries carried the painting off to Paris and it took Waterloo to get it back. Bourgeois entrepreneurs sold a British collector the side-panels, which ended up in Germany. A long tug-of-war ensued as the panels and the rest of the painting went back and forth between 1914 and 1945. Finally the American Army found the work, side-panels and all, in some Tyrolean salt mines and returned it to Ghent, with Adam and Eve once again blissfully naked.

The artistic jewel of its interior is **The Adoration of the Mystic Lamb** (1432), a huge altar painting by Jan van Eyck (with possible additions by brother Hubert) in the baptis-

tery. This monumental work celebrates a church triumphant with superb portraits of the donors, saints, prophets and princes of the church surrounding the hallowed Lamb, symbol of redemption, above the fountain of life. The landscape is a botanists' delight, depicting 42 different plants, while the "Jerusalem" of the background has been identified as a composite skyline of Utrecht, Bruges, Mainz and Cologne.

Ghent has two great old castles. **Geraard de Duivelsteen** (Castle of Gerard the Devil) overlooks the River Schelde on Bauwens square. This forbidding 13th-century construction, known in its time for the nasty torture chambers, now houses the dusty state archives of western Flanders. The **Gravensteen,** moated castle of the counts of Flanders, is perhaps marginally more attractive, more varied in its design which ranged over the 9th to the 12th centuries, but it can boast just as unpleasant a history as old Gerard's place. Take a look at the dungeons and the charming museum of instruments of torture, with strait-jackets, head-shrinkers (in iron), balls-and-chains, ankle-braces and leg-irons to fit all sizes. There's a nice view from the terrace at the top, where they launched their cannonballs and poured the boiling oil.

In the same vein, you can admire the **Dulle Griet** (Angry Maggie), an enormous 16-tonne iron cannon, displayed near the Vrijdagmarkt (Friday market). In the 15th century this monster—now surrounded by a jolly little hedge—used to fire stone balls that weighed 750 pounds. Its destructive power may well have inspired Brueghel's violent painting of war of the same name on view in the Mayer van den Bergh Museum in Antwerp (see p. 64).

To restore your peace of mind, visit one of the many colourful **markets** that Ghent has to offer almost every day of the week all over town—flowers, birds, fruits and vegetables, domestic pets, poultry, cattle, and a lively flea-market on the Beverhout square beside St.-Jacobskerk, the city's oldest church.

Of Ghent's many museums, here are the most interesting: **The Museum voor Volkskunde** (Folklore) in a 14th-century children's home, Kraanlei 63, offers an intimate glimpse of the past, with a series of 19th-century Flemish interiors. The outstanding works of the **Museum voor Schone Kunsten**

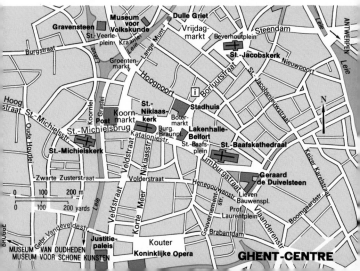

MUSEUM VOOR VOLKSKUNDE GENT

Ghent's Folklore Museum is housed in a 14th-century children's home.

(Fine Arts), on De Liemaecke-replein 3, are two paintings by Hieronymus Bosch—*Saint Jerome* and *The Bearing of the Cross*, in which Jesus is almost lost amid the ugly, hateful crowd surrounding him. There is an excellent tapestry room displaying works from Brussels' golden era of the 17th century. But the loveliest museum in Ghent, **Museum van Oudheden** (Godshuizenlaan 2) is housed in the exquisite medieval Abbey of Bijloke and contains a fascinating collection of old artefacts. Be sure to visit the beautiful gabled refectory and wander around the restored Renaissance garden, leaving Angry Maggie far, far away.

Bruges

Pop. 120,000

Bruges *(Brugge* in Flemish*)* is, quite simply, the prettiest town in Belgium and one of the prettiest in Europe. It's a town to walk in, to take a boat-ride in, to do everything in leisurely fashion. It's a town where civilization takes on a quieter, more dignified, more reassuring meaning. Walk around Bruges, past the old houses, along the banks of the canals, stand on the bridge over the Minnewater and look back at the Begijnhof, the cathedral and beyond that to the belfry and the Town Hall, all so solid, peaceful, immovable, and you may ask, if you've had a difficult day, why can't the whole world be like this?

This air of blessed apartness did not come easily. Things began well enough, with the Zwin inlet making Bruges a desirable protected port for international trade in the Middle Ages. Attractive enough for the king of France, Philip the Fair, to grab it from the count of Flanders in 1301. In fact, when Philip arrived in town, the ladies of Bruges turned out so elegantly to receive him that his wife threw a jealous tantrum. But the men of Bruges didn't want any part of the French. Their revolt against the invaders in May 1302 took the form of a tongue-twister. Anyone who couldn't pronounce their war cry *"Schild en vriend"* (shield and friend) with the right guttural turns had to be a Frenchman and was slaughtered, 1,400 of them in one night.

Thereafter, Bruges came into its own as a port, a transit for the great Hanseatic League, shipping coal, wool and cheese from England, wine from Germany, furs from Russia, metal from Poland and the Balkans, spices from the Orient. The prosperity lasted until the end of the 15th century, then the Zwin silted up, the Flemish cloth industry collapsed, trade routes changed and Bruges was eclipsed by Antwerp. It slumbered until the end of the 19th century, admired only by lugubrious Romantic writers who loved the melancholy decadence of "Bruges-la-Morte". The building of the port of Zeebrugge in 1907, linked by canal to Bruges, brought about a spectacular revival and the town has been able to face the 20th century with optimism without losing touch with its proud and poetic past.

If you're coming to Bruges by car, park it at your hotel or

some other safe place such as the Markt, and forget it. There are just two ways to see the town—on foot and in a boat— and you should try both. Boats leave from four embarcation points, the Vismarkt, Rozenhoedkaai, the Dyver and the Gruuthusebrug, all south and south-west of the Town Hall. The half-hour boat-trips, which run all day long, are the perfect introduction to this dreamy town, getting you in tune with Bruges' gentler pace.

When you're ready to walk, start at the **Markt**, the main square or Grand-Place, so characteristic of Belgian cities. In the centre is a 19th-century monument to Pieter de Coninck and Jan Breydel, who led the revolt against the French in 1302. They were defending the hard-earned privileges of the corporations and the trade profits, symbolized by the magnificent weathered-brick **Halle** (covered market) and **Belfort** (belfry) that dominate the square today. The 13th-century Halle and belfry have survived the town's ups and downs in shining splendour. Above the entrance to the belfry is a balcony from which the magistrates read their proclamations, often new laws, before the people summoned by the great bells. You

can see these bells if you climb all the way to the top (366 steps). In summer there are morning and evening concerts.

Opposite the Halle, on the north side of the square, are some fine corporation houses from the 17th century, the best perhaps being the House of the Fishmongers with anchors decorating its gabled façade.

The **Town Hall** (Stadhuis) of Bruges, begun in 1376, set the architectural pattern for Flanders' citadels of municipal power—its square is still known as Burg or fortress. The building thrusts uncompromisingly upwards with elegant turrets, tall, narrow windows bearing the coats of arms of surrounding towns subject to Bruges' domination in the Middle Ages, slim, erect statuary of historic heroes. Every line in the structure proclaims the town's imperturbable civic pride. There's a balcony on the right where the counts of Flanders came to take their oath of fidelity to the town's inalienable civic liberties. Inside, on the ground floor, you'll see sculptures of the biblical proph-

Bruges is always a study in colour from the brickwork to the parasols.

ets and get the feeling that the town's aldermen identified very strongly with these formidable forefathers. If you have any doubts left, visit the imposing 14th-century **Gothic Room** on the first floor with its vaulted wooden ceiling. The place brims over with dignity.

Across a canal is the **Gerechtshof** (Law Courts), formerly the palace of the Free Council of Bruges. Although it was transformed in the 18th century, there remains an attractive 16th-century façade overlooking the canal. You should also visit the Council Chamber for its splendid Renaissance fireplace of dark marble, oak and white alabaster. It was built to celebrate Charles V's victory of 1525 over François I at Pavia. Charles himself has pride of place among the sculptures, brandishing his sword amidst life-size statues of his ancestors, Ferdinand and Isabella of Spain to the left, Maximilian of Austria and Marie of Burgundy to the right. An alabaster frieze of the biblical story of Susannah and the old men adorns the mantlepiece, and just below are three ornately carved copper rings which the aldermen held on to while dangling their muddy boots to dry off near the fire.

Your best view of the Law Courts' 16th-century façade is from the Steenhouwersdijk next to the still operative fish market *(Vismarkt)*. To the east is the lovely **Groene Rei** (Green Quay) with its tree-lined gardens bordering the canal and its rickety-looking
76

—but in fact sturdy—humpbacked bridges. This is a place to sit and savour. Look back to the great towers of the St.-Salvator cathedral, of Onze Lieve Vrouwekerk (church of Notre-Dame) and of the belfry, and then relax among the quaint little dwellings for the elderly, **De Pelikaan** (1714), named after the bird you'll find in a bas-relief over the main entrance.

Walk back—slowly, remember—to the **Rozenhoedkaai** (Rosary Quay), pause a while on the bridge *(Sint-Jan Nepomucenusbrug)* commemorating the throwing of the Archbishop of Prague into the River Moldau. And on to the **Dyver,** each stretch of tree-shaded canal bank offering a new, gently changing perspective of intimate gabled houses, ivy-covered bridges and that public, civic, ecclesiastical skyline behind to remind you occasionally of the outside world.

The Dyver takes you to the **Groeninge Museum,** a superb collection of early Flemish painting, mostly from the 15th-century Primitive School of which Bruges was a celebrated centre. **Jan van Eyck** is represented by two master works, *The Madonna and the Canon van der Paele* (1436) and *Margareta van Eyck* (1439), a marvellously frank,

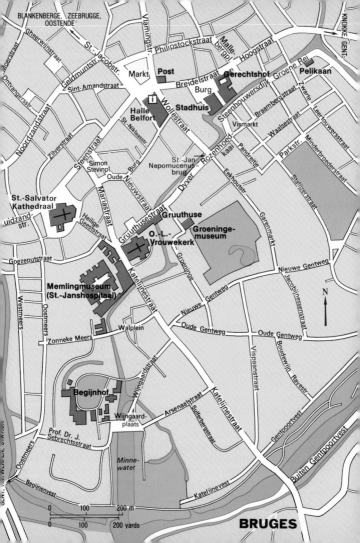

BLANKENBERGE, ZEEBRUGGE, OOSTENDE

KNOKKE, GENT

Gheerwijnstraat
St.-Jacobstr.
Vlamingstr.
Philipstockstraat
Malle bergpl.
Hoogstraat

Moerstraat
Geldmuntstr.
Markt
Post
Breidelstraat
Burg
Gerechtshof
Groene Rei
Pelikaan

Ontvangersstr.
Sint-Amandstraat
i
Wollestraat
Stadhuis
Steenbouwersdijk
zwarte Leertouwersstraat

Noordzandstraat
Zilverstraat
Halle Belfort
St.-Niklaasstr.
Vismarkt
Braambergstraat
Waalsestraat
Leertouwersstraat

Steenstraat
Simon Stevinpl.
Burg
Oude Nieuwstraat
St.-Jan Nepomucenus-brug
Rozenhoed kaai
Pandreitje
Parkstr.
Minderbroederstraat

St.-Salvator Kathedraal
Heilige Geeststraat
Mariastraat
Gruuthusestraat
Dyver
Eekhoutstr.
Garenmarkt
Stalijnstraat

uidzand str.
Gruuthuse
O.-L.-Vrouwekerk
Groeninge-museum
Goezeputstraat

Memlingmuseum (St.-Jnshospitaal)
Katelijnestraat
Groeninge
Nieuwe Gentweg
Jacobinessenstraat
N

Westmeers
Oostmeers
Walplein
Nieuwe Gentweg
Oude Gentweg
Oude Gentweg
Vispaanstraat

Zonneke Meers
Winnaardstraat

Begijnhof
Wijngaard-plaats
Arsenaalstraat
Suikerbergstraat
Katelijnestraat
Boudewijn Ravestr.
Gentpoortvest

Prof. Dr. J. Sebrechtsstraat
Minne-water
Katelijnevest
Buiten Gentpoortvest

Begijnenvest
Oostmeers

0   100   200 m
0   100   200 yards

BRUGES

unidealized portrait of his wife. Other important paintings include a moving *Death of the Virgin* by **Hugo van der Goes;** *The Annunciation* in two separate panels depicting Gabriel and Mary, by **Hans Memling,** as well as his great Moreel triptych showing St. Christopher carrying Jesus, with side panels of the prolific Burgomaster Moreel and his wife with their 5 sons and 11, yes 11, daughters; a *Baptism of Christ* triptych by Gerard David; and *The Last Judgment* by Hieronymus Bosch. You can follow the whole career of Jan van Eyck, who spent his adult life in Bruges, in an excellent slide presentation.

Next to the museum is the fine old **Gruuthuse** (House of Groats—the fermented barley used in the brewing of beer), now a museum of arts and crafts. The walk continues through to the church of **Onze Lieve Vrouw,** a little austere in the framework of Bruges architecture but worth your attention for an early sculpture of Michelangelo, *The Virgin and the Child,* in the chapel of the Virgin. The Lanchals Chapel contains the tombs of Charles the Bold and Marie of Burgundy. Her death in a riding accident in 1482 left the Low Countries in the hands of the Habsburgs. You should also look for two fine paintings by the 15th-century Cologne master Stefan Lochner, *The Annunciation* and *The Adoration of the Magi.*

The **St.-Salvator** cathedral suffered through four great fires in the 800 years of its history, plus the ravages of the Calvinists, so that little of its old glory remains. But the choir still has some beautifully carved 15th-century stalls, fine Brussels tapestries and an impressive 16th-century tombstone for the Bishop Carondelet. The cathedral's museum includes two noteworthy paintings by Dirk Bouts and Hugo van der Goes.

Bruges is almost as proud of Hans Memling as Antwerp is of Rubens and a **Memling Museum** is installed in the old hospital of St. John *(St.-Jans-hospitaal).* Memling moved to Bruges from his native Mainz and did most of his important work in the city. The central piece is the *Reliquary of St. Ursula,* six paintings on a sculpted wood casket in the form of a Gothic chapel. They tell the story of Ursula's trip with 11,000 virgins from England to Rome, where she was received by the pope. On the way home, she and her girls were massacred by the pagans of Cologne. Memling's noble use of light and colour can also be seen in the magnificent altarpiece *Mystical Marriage of St. Catherine*, with side panels devoted to St. John the Evangelist and St. John the Baptist, the hospital's patrons.

Walk down the lively shopping street, Katelijnestraat, till the Wijngaardstraat turns to the right onto a little square where you can watch lace makers working on their doorsteps on sunny days. Cross the hump-backed bridge to the 18th-century gateway of the **Begijnhof**, a nunnery founded in 1245 by Margaret of Constantinople. Suddenly you're in another of those places where you feel far, far away from it all—though after a while in Bruges you begin to forget what it is you left behind. For centuries this blessed haven of peace housed the Beguines, pious women who devoted their lives to prayer and such delicate industry as lace-making or weaving. In 1930, the last of the Beguines died and Benedictine nuns took their place, but continued the tradition of tranquil

The best way to enjoy the lovely weathered façades is from a boat.

labour and meditation. Today you can walk among the trees —daffodils in springtime—and visit one of the little white houses of the cloister, a spartanly furnished bedroom, living-room with religious paintings, and a kitchen overlooking a small garden with a well.

If your own meditation tends more to the gently profane than to the sacred, your visit to Bruges will end blissfully at the **Minnewater** (Lake of Love) south of the Begijnhof. If the latter is blessed, the Minnewater is most definitely charmed by the most benign of pagan spirits, a cool expanse of still water, the perfect place for quiet walks, for whispered poems, for lying on the grass and staring up through the trees at nothing in particular as the swans glide silently by.

At the southern end of the Minnewater is a bridge where the Ghent Canal begins and next to the bridge is a 15th-century gunpowder house, for the defence of the old ramparts, but today you don't really care to know about things like that.

The Begijnhof takes you back to another, more peaceful epoch, when Memling painted this Madonna.

The Coast

If you've been running around a lot, you'll be ready for a rest on the beach. Belgium's coast on the North Sea is as bracing and healthy as any in Europe. Because of the iodine in the salty air, they say, the suntan you get on the beaches between Ostend and Knokke-Heist lasts longer than the more expensive brand from the Côte d'Azur.

Ostend (*Oostende/Ostende;* pop. 70,000) is a jolly seaside

The Swan Song Goes On

In 1488 the people of Bruges rebelled against Archduke Maximilian of Austria and imprisoned him and his counsellor Pieter Lanchals, whose head they chopped off. To avoid a similar fate, Maximilian promised to satisfy the citizens' complaints and was released. He immediately ordered that the people of Bruges keep in perpetuity a flock of swans on their waters in expiation of the death of Lanchals (whose name meant "long neck" and whose coat of arms bore a swan). Unlike Maximilian, the people kept their side of the bargain, and today the swans still parade with a B for Bruges and their date of birth marked on their beaks.

town with a whiff of the naughty nineties and the Belle Epoque along its Albert I Promenade, from the Kursaal (Casino) to the Hippodrome, a whiff that mixes pungently with oysters, cockles, mussels and suntan lotion. The beaches have splendid old-fashioned sunbathing-huts, parasols and deckchairs lined up in colourful phalanxes that look, from the promenade, like battalions of toy soldiers. Only the bikinis betray the fact that this is not 1900.

Boat lovers will enjoy wandering around the **port,** amateur fishermen can marvel as the fleet unloads its catch early in the morning at the **minque** (fish market), where 50 million kilos of fish are sold each year. The sole are especially good.

If you haven't had your fill of culture, plan a visit to the fine arts museum at the **Feestpaleis** for a look at the weird and wonderful work of Ostend's own James Ensor. The extensive collection—20 paintings, 80 drawings and over 100 etchings of vibrant satire—captures that special Belgian mixture of the grim and the hilarious. **Ensor's home** *(Ensorhuis)* at Vlaanderenstraat 27 has been turned into a museum recreating his studio on the top floor, complete with some

of his favourite grotesque masks.

But for a quiet swim, move on to **Bredene,** where you'll find the most beautiful sand dunes, ideal for camping, fishing and impromptu dancing by moonlight. People preferring family hotels go on to **Blankenberge,** with all the fun of the fair at the Luna Park. On rainy days, there's always the aquarium.

The chic spot on the coast is **Knokke-Heist**—elegant bou-

Belgians claim their seaside gives you a terrific suntan. Even if you find this hard to swallow, you'll love the bracing air of Knokke's beach.

tiques, luxurious hotels, swank nightclubs. The casino, it seems, has the biggest chandelier in Europe, made of Venetian crystal with 2,000 lights. And the number 13 wins at the roulette tables just as often as it does anywhere else. Further east, in the exclusive district known as the Zoute, you'll find some dazzling resort villas surrounded by beautiful gardens, immaculately barbered lawns protected by the strictest of laws to keep out philistine property-developers.

Between Knokke and the Dutch border is the delightful natural reserve of the **Zwin**, a stretch of 360 acres of sand dunes and grassland reclaimed from the sea when Bruges lost its inland waterway (see p. 57). Open to the public, the Zwin shelters some 300 species of birds, including rare storks, herons and geese saved from extinction by the resident ornithologists. The birds can best be observed in springtime, the countless varieties of flowers and plants in the summer, and any time of the year you can see just as many wild rabbits as the wild rabbits can muster.

What to Do

Entertainment

Music plays an important part in Brussels' cultural life and **opera** is of a high international standard at the historic Théâtre de la Monnaie. Reversing the usual trend of Belgian artists seeking fame in France, the great Marseilles choreographer Maurice Béjart made

Brussels his home for some 20 years. His innovative **ballet** troupe attracted fans from all over the world and created a tradition of the art of dance that will certainly continue. Orchestral **concerts** and recitals are held at the Palais des Beaux-Arts and outdoors on the Grand-Place during the spring and summer.

Theatre, both classical and experimental, has over 30 stages to choose from in the capital. Typically the Théâtre National on the Place Rogier has a repertory (in French) that includes Harold Pinter, Samuel Beckett and Tennessee Williams as well as Molière and Maeterlinck.

A special Brussels attraction is the at once highly sophisticated and robustly popular **puppet theatre,** Théâtre de Toone, on an impasse off the Petite rue des Bouchers. This tiny theatre with over 150 years of tradition has a programme that offers *Macbeth, Faust* and *The Count of Monte Cristo* full of boisterous humour and gripping pathos, delivered in a mixture of classical French and Brussels patois. The exquisite costumes and broad gestures make it a joy for the least linguistically endowed adult or child.

Nightclubs and **discothèques** are scattered all over town, most of them with the longevity and reproductive ability of butterflies and mushrooms. You'll find the fashionable ones around the Avenue Louise and Chaussée de Waterloo, more discreet ones around the Sablon and the more brassy around the Place de Brouckère. On the coast your best bet is at Knokke.

Cinemas in Brussels and elsewhere in Belgium have the great advantage of the country's bilingualism making it necessary for all films to be played in their original version with subtitles, rather than the increasingly clumsy dubbed versions too often found in other countries. The Palais des Beaux-Arts has an excellent *cinémathèque* of "collectors' items" open to the public.

Festivals

But entertainment in Belgium also means the enormously popular festivals, celebrations of folklore often derived from an obscure historical or religious event that makes a good

Brussels has become an important centre for ballet.

excuse today for a procession, **85**

some fireworks, dancing, dressing up, a party for everybody.

Brussels' own biggest festivity is the *Ommegang* (see pp. 27–28), on the first Tuesday and Thursday in July, when the flags and banners of the corporations and the old Chambers of Rhetoric are paraded to recreate the pageant which Charles V witnessed in 1549. The Grand-Place is also the site of a score of other festivities, a Begonia Festival which covers the square in a fantastic carpet of flowers, open-air theatre performances, concerts, rock, dances, anything the city fathers can lay their hands on to keep the party going through spring and summer. For some reason they even plant the May Tree, *Meyboom,* on August 9.

Along the coast, **Blankenberge** has a Port Festival in May or June and a mass to bless the sea in July. On the last Sunday in August it holds a flower procession. Mardi Gras is a big occasion here, as throughout Belgium.

Ostend holds a big charity ball known as the Ball of the Dead Rat, at the Casino with costumes and masks inspired by James Ensor, one of the ball's originators. On the same night the competing Shrimp Ball, more popular and boisterous, is held in the fishermen's district, preceded by a grand procession. Ostend's mass for the sea is held on the last Sunday in June. Ostend also has an international festival through July and August.

Bruges' great festivity, held on Ascension Day in May, is the *Heilig-Bloedprocessie* (Procession of the Holy Blood), honouring a relic said to contain drops of Christ's blood brought back from Jerusalem after the Crusades by the

count of Flanders in 1150. Recently, experts established that the relic, of dubious origin, in fact came from Constantinople 100 years later, but the procession still goes on. Bruges celebrates Mardi Gras on the preceding Saturday with a procession and dancing in the streets. The canals are illuminated on weekends through the month of May and then throughout the summer. There's a fine sound-and-light show held at the Gruuthuse from the beginning of July to mid-September.

Belgium's national holiday is July 21 and then everybody celebrates, more or less.

The people of Brussels love dressing in exotic costumes and grotesque masks for their myriad festivals. This is the Fête des Géants (Giants).

Shopping

In these days of standardization and ever more efficient import and export facilities, it is difficult to pinpoint the distinctive present you can buy in Brussels and won't find anywhere else. But there are still a few specialities to look out for.

Although inflation has sent costs sky-high and Brussels' international community has pushed the prices even higher, it is Belgium's own products that offer the most attractive prices. You'll discover this is true both in the elegant boutiques of Avenue Louise and the Galeries St-Hubert or in the more popular shops of the Marolles and the department stores on Rue Neuve and Boulevard Adolphe Max.

In the general movement to rediscover the old arts and crafts, **lace** is coming back into vogue and the best is to be found in Brussels and Bruges. Much of it is machine-made,

copies of old patterns, but you can still find hand-made work of exquisite quality, as well as innovative patterns in modern styles by the new generation.

Tapestry is also a machine-made business these days but, if you're prepared to pay the price for the real thing, there are still some hand-made pieces to be found around the Sablon antique dealers and art galleries—expensive but still a better buy than in Paris or London.

Shops in the Belgian capital vary from chic Art Nouveau façades to pavement stalls in the Marolles.

Glassware and **crystal** from Liège (Val St-Lambert), Charleroi and Malines are on sale in the fine shops on the Avenue Louise and the *grands boulevards*. **Pewter** is brought in from Halle. Fine **leather** goods are a Brussels speciality.

If you're thinking of making **89**

a **gold** or **silver** investment in something other than ingots and coins, Brussels is of course still a great centre for jewellery and other pieces of fine craftsmanship. While you're up in this bracket, you might want to pause in your sightseeing in Antwerp for a side-trip to the **diamond** market. They have a fabulous selection of the world's most exorbitant trinkets.

More modest but no less artistic, if you can lug it home, is

Lace is still a proud tradition of Belgian craftsmanship. You can get both hand- and machine-made.

the finely wrought **ironware** from both Brussels and Antwerp. They make lovely reproductions of medieval firescreens and you might even come across an original—though you can be sure the dealer will know its proper price. Then again...

Wooden toys are still a flourishing craft in Spa and Verviers and on sale in the capital.

All these products, of course, are available brand new, but **antique** originals can also be seen both in the experts' shops on the Sablon and at the flea markets—in the Marolles on the Place du Jeu de Balle, in Antwerp at St. Jacob's Church, and in Ghent on the Beverhoutsplein. Don't be afraid to bargain. It's expected of you.

Belgium offers a tempting array of **eatable souvenirs.** Most famous are the custommade *pralines,* luscious filled chocolates. From the coast comes a hard sweet, *babeluttes.* There are also a variety of typical biscuits—almond, honey and spice *(speculoos).*

The **markets** are a delight wherever you go—the bird and flower markets on Brussels' Grand-Place, the markets for absoutely everything in Ghent, from chickens, to flowers, to cattle (see p. 71).

Sports

Belgium is not ashamed of its description as *"le plat pays"* (the flat country). This topographical fact has been turned into a national sport—and one that visitors can happily take to—**cycling.** Even if you're not up to Tour de France standard (which many Belgians most definitely are), you can buy yourself a little cap, strap a bag on your back and take off on your own road race. Bicycles are for hire at the railway station in almost every town, especially at the seaside where it's the preferred means of transport. In Ostend, they seem to favour tricycles for two. One of the best rides is from Knokke-Heist along the sea-wall to the Dutch border and back. All the Brussels parks have special bicycle paths. (See also p. 106.)

If cycling is too slow for you, another great sport on the Belgian coast is **sand-sailing.** With a good wind blowing in from the North Sea, you can whip along the beach at fantastic speeds. You may capsize but at least you won't drown.

Water sports are popular, from the sedate pedalo to the more adventurous wind-surfing and water-skiing, the latter not just at the seaside but also **91**

To go **fishing** inland, you need a permit (easily obtained from the post office). On the coast you can wangle your way onto the fishing boats at Ostend and Zeebrugge for deepsea fishing. Try to catch yourself a delicious sole. The rivers and canals are well stocked with trout, carp, pike, chubb and roach.

The Forest of Soignes is the perfect place for **horse-riding.** The Brussels Tourist Office will give you information about where to hire a horse for the day and also about the organized "Belgium on Horseback" tours that last from 2 to 12 days.

Hikers can follow a network of marked trails across the countryside. Contact the Comité National Belge des Sentiers de Grande Randonnée (B.P. 10, 4000 Liège) for details.

Golf courses can be found in Brussels at Tervuren, in Ghent at Sint-Martens-Latem, in Antwerp at Kapellenbos, in Ostend at Klemskerke, and in Knokke-Heist.

Tennis, which has long been a private affair in Belgium, is opening up to the public now and your hotel or the tourist office should be able to help you get a court. You'll probably find whites de rigueur.

on the River Schelde at Antwerp. It is easy to rent boats for sailing at Bruges' port at Zeebrugge or at Blankenberge and Ostend. If you like a nice simple rowboat, try the lakes in the Brussels parks of Bois de la Cambre, Woluwe and Tervuren, or the Lac de Genval in **92** the Forêt de Soignes.

The best spectator sports are **soccer**—with a world-class Brussels team at Anderlecht, **motor racing** for the Grand Prix at Francorchamps, near Spa, and **horse-racing,** which takes place in the Brussels area at Groenendael and Boitsfort, trotting at Sterrebeek and steeplechase at Waregem. At Ostend the racing is at the Hippodrome Wellington—at least one place where the winner at Waterloo is more celebrated than the loser.

Outdoor sports are at a premium. Try boating out at Knokke or the horse-riding in the Cambre woods.

Dining in Brussels

Let's deal right away with one of the facile clichés about the Belgians—that they eat nothing but mussels and chips (French fries) washed down with beer. While this is far from the whole truth, it is worth stating for the record that the mussels are excellent, the chips the best in Europe and the beer rich and varied enough to rival the other great beer centres of Germany and Czechoslovakia.

The **mussels** *(moules**)* fished from the North Sea are brought in fresh every day to Brussels. Served steamed, in a seasoned broth, they're a meal in themselves. The **chips** *(frites)* are crispy and succulent, fried once quickly and then dipped again in boiling oil to give them the special crackly finish insisted on by any connoisseur who knows a good chip from a floppy one.

The **beer** isn't just beer. It's the national ambrosia. In a country where the average per capita consumption runs almost 150 litres a year (compared with 45 in France), brewing has become as fine an art as the making of a great Bordeaux. The barley and hops that go into the malting and yeasting are picked and sorted with a refinement of technique that goes back to the monasteries which controlled a beer monopoly in the Middle Ages.

Beer is Good for You

It all started in the 11th century with good old St. Arnold. The pope sent him back to his native Flanders to protect the people against a pillaging baron and his armies. Arnold did the job so well that the people asked him to stay and found an abbey at Oudenburg not far from Bruges. There he noticed that the people were dying like flies from drinking the polluted water of the local river, while the beer-drinking layabouts were the picture of health. He summoned his congregation to the town brewery where he plunged his ceremonial cross into the vat and told them: "Don't drink the water, drink the beer." The brewing process had of course killed off all the microbes in the water, added healthy proteins, vitamins and mineral salts, and everybody thrived. Especially the brewers, who made Arnold their patron saint.

---

* For Flemish terms, consult the Menu Reader (pp. 99–100). And for a comprehensive guide to dining in Belgium, see the Berlitz EUROPEAN MENU READER.

Restaurants

Brussels has no inferiority complex towards Paris when it comes to cuisine. The Belgians' indomitable taste for the good life demands of their restaurants the very highest quality, drawing on the great traditions of neighbouring French cuisine, but adding ingenious new touches and rich variations derived from regional products.

The best Brussels restaurants are certainly expensive, but gourmets and gourmands alike will get their money's worth. One of the great assets is the way the managers, cooks and waiters take pride in what they serve, whether in the simplest bistrot or tavern or the most luxurious establishment.

For light meals, there are many taverns and cafés where you can simply have a glass of beer or wine with some cold cuts of meat, sausage, pâté or cheese and a small salad.

While the more chic restaurants have an elegance that demands that men wear at least a jacket if not a tie and that women show appropriate taste, too, the atmosphere in most popular bistrots is very

With a Belgian's huge appetite, these lobsters may be one serving.

relaxed. The accent is always on the enjoyment.

In general, portions are enormous and you will usually be offered more. The trick is to take a modest amount the first time and then you can keep everybody happy by digging in heartily for the second helping. Very frequently an order of pâté, for instance, comes not in the form of one slice on the plate, but the whole terrine with a knife and smiling instructions to help yourself. Soup bowls tend to be quite simply bottomless.

There have been many attempts to explain the enormous appetites of the Belgians,

the most convincing being that they combine the natural sturdy capacity of other northern European peoples with the stimulation of Gallic finesse in what's placed before them.

Local Specialities
Among **hors d'œuvres,** there is of course a beer soup *(soupe à la bière)* with chicken stock and onions; a kind of cold pâté of veal, pork and rabbit known as *potjesvlees;* and *flamiche,* a savoury cheese pie with leeks or onions; *tomate aux crevettes,* tomato filled with shrimps and mayonnaise, and *croquettes de crevette;* fine smoked ham, *jambon d'Ardennes;* and the famous oysters *(huîtres),* today actually from Zeeland.

The best-known **main dish** is probably *waterzooi,* a chicken (or sometimes fish) stewed with whites of leeks, bouillon, cream and egg yolks. *Anguille au vert* is eel flavoured with any number of green herbs, but most popularly with sorrel, sage and parsley. The *carbonnade* consists of pieces of lean beef browned in a pan and then cooked in a casserole with lots of onions and—beer. Another Flemish stew is *hochepot,* a pot-au-feu using oxtail or pigs' trotters, ears and snout. *Lapin à la flamande* is made of pieces of rabbit marinated in beer and vinegar and then braised in onions and prunes —delicious. *Coucous* are not cuckoos but a variety of chicken. Excellent game—venison *(chevreuil),* pheasant *(faisan)* and hare *(lièvre)*—comes from the Ardennes.

Vegetable dishes include *chou rouge à la flamande,* red cabbage, cooked with apples, onions, red wine and vinegar; *chicorée* (or *chicon*), braised endives, often served *gratinée au four* (baked with cheese and ham); in spring *asperges de Malines,* local white asparagus dressed with melted butter and crumbled hard-cooked egg; and, naturally enough, *choux de Bruxelles* (brussels sprouts) often prepared with chestnuts, pieces of bacon and cooked lightly in goose-fat.

Among local **cheeses** are the very strong *remoudou,* the *djotte de Nivelles* and cream cheeses from Brussels. And look for the two-layered pancake with a cheese-filling, known simply as a *double.*

Grapes and strawberries cultivated in hot-houses appear on restaurant menus all year long.

Speculoos gingerbreads come in every imaginable size and shape.

Waffles *(gaufres)* are the best-known **dessert** of Belgian origin, but you should also try the *crêpes aux pommes* (apple pancakes), *beignets de Bruxelles*, a sort of doughnut or fritter, *tarte au riz*, rice tart, *manons*, chocolate filled with fresh cream, and the famous *speculoos*, spicy gingerbreads cut in the shape of kings, queens, bishops and knights.

And for those whose sweet tooth hasn't been satisfied yet, consider *pralines*, local chocolates of great subtlety in flavour and variety. They are exported all over the world, but the best selection remains back in Brussels.

If you're looking for a **snack** to tide you over till the next meal, rest assured Brussels will not disappoint you. The famous *frites* are available day and night at special *friture* stands—served in paper cones with salt and mayonnaise. Another street speciality is *caricoles* (sea snails). You eat them piping hot with a cup of the spicy broth they were cooked in.

Drinks

With almost everything, you drink St. Arnold's favourite beverage—Belgian beer. There are four basic brews in the Brussels area, all made by a process of spontaneous fermentation, i.e. without yeast: the *Gueuze*, slightly sour in taste with a fine head of foam when poured; as opposed to the *Lambic* brewed in Brueghel's old stomping-grounds in the Senne valley south-west of Brussels, a young beer without foam but plenty of strength; the *Faro* is a variety of *Lambic* with a much lower alcohol content, more difficult to find these days; lastly, the bizarre *Kriek*, a reddish beer with the fruity taste of the cherries added during the *Lambic's* fermentation. In and around Antwerp you'll find the *trappiste*, a dark malt beer, as well as *pils*, a light beer brewed locally from fermentation at low temperatures (also available in Brussels, of course).

Belgium does not produce any wines of note, but the selections of French and German wines are often superior to what you might find in equivalent establishments in the countries of origin. The Belgians seem to take pride in making an extra effort, perhaps to show that they appreciate even better than the natives what makes a good Bordeaux or Mosel wine.

An oddity of Belgian bars is that they do not serve strong alcoholic drinks like whisky and liqueurs—of course available in restaurants with your meals. Be sure to try the local gin, a little sweet, known as *péguet*.

To Help You Order...

Could we have a table?	**Pouvons-nous avoir une table?**	*Heeft u een tafel voor ons?*
Do you have a set menu?	**Avez-vous un menu du jour?**	*Heeft u een menu van de dag?*
I'd like a/an/some...	**J'aimerais...**	*Ik zou graag... willen hebben.*
beer	**une bière**	*een pils*
butter	**du beurre**	*boter*
bread	**du pain**	*brood*
cheese	**du fromage**	*kaas*
coffee	**un café**	*koffie*
egg(s)	**un œuf(s)**	*een ei(eren)*
ice-cream	**une glace**	*ijs*
meat	**de la viande**	*vlees*
menu	**la carte**	*een menu*
milk	**du lait**	*melk*
mineral water	**de l'eau minérale**	*mineraal water*
salad	**une salade**	*sla*
sugar	**du sucre**	*de suiker*
tea	**du thé**	*thee*
wine	**du vin**	*wijn*

...and Read the Menu in French

agneau	lamb	**lapin**	rabbit
anguille	eel	**lièvre**	hare
bœuf	beef	**moules**	mussels
canard	duck	**oie**	goose
champignons	mushrooms	**petits pois**	peas
chou	cabbage	**pommes**	apples
chou-fleur	cauliflower	**pommes**	potatoes
choux de	brussels	**de terre**	
Bruxelles	sprouts	**porc**	pork
crevettes	shrimps	**poulet**	chicken
endives	chicory	**pruneaux**	prunes
(chicon)	(endive)	**raisins**	grapes
épinards	spinach	**ris de veau**	sweetbreads
faisan	pheasant	**riz**	rice
foie	liver	**rognons**	kidney
fraises	strawberries	**saucisse/**	sausage
haricots	green beans	**saucisson**	
verts		**truite**	trout
jambon	ham	**veau**	veal
langue	tongue	**volaille**	poultry

...and in Flemish

aardappelen	potatoes	**pruimen**	prunes
aardbeien	strawberries	**rijst**	rice
bloemkool	cauliflower	**rodekool**	red cabbage
druiven	grapes	**rundvlees**	beef
eend	duck	**spruitjes**	brussels
forel	trout		sprouts
frieten	chips (French	**tong (vis)**	sole (fish)
	fries)	**tong**	tongue (meat)
garnalen	shrimps	**(vlees)**	
haas	hare	**uien**	onions
kip	chicken	**varkensvlees**	pork
konijn	rabbit	**witloof**	chicory
mosselen	mussels		(endive)
100 **paling**	eel	**worst**	sausage

BLUEPRINT for a Perfect Trip

How to Get There

Whether you're making a short trip across the North Sea or coming from the other side of the world, the choice of routes and fares is so varied that the services of a knowledgeable travel agent are indispensible.

BY AIR

Brussels airport (see also p. 105) is linked by direct flights from almost all European and many North-American cities. Travellers from further afield may have to connect via Paris, Amsterdam or London.

Enquire about reductions on scheduled flights, like for example:

- for stays of fixed duration determined in advance
- for children and students under 12, 21 or 26
- for spouses
- for senior citizens
- for families

A fly-and-drive arrangement (with hire car at the airport) is particularly interesting if you plan to see the environs of Brussels, too.

BY SEA AND ROAD

The *Queen Elizabeth 2* makes about ten return trips a year from Southampton in southern England to New York. Consult your travel agent for the latest schedule.

The jet foil (passengers only) goes from London to Ostend in 4 hours. Slightly longer, but with car-carrying facilities, are the ferry and hovercraft crossings between Dover and Felixstowe to Ostend and Zeebrugge. If you prefer a shorter sea crossing and a longer drive, you could take the hovercraft or ferry from Dover to Calais or Boulogne (France).

BY COACH

There are direct coach services from major European cities and from London and several provincial centres in Britain to Brussels.

BY RAIL

Overseas visitors who intend to do a lot of rail travelling around continental Europe may be interested in purchasing a *Eurailpass*. This flat-rate, unlimited-mileage ticket is valid for first-class travel practically anywhere in western Europe except Great Britain. Anyone under 26 can get the second-class *Eurail Youthpass*. These tickets must be bought before you leave your country of residence.

The *Rail Europ S* (senior) card, obtainable before departure only, entitles senior citizens to purchase train tickets for European destinations at reduced prices.

Any family of at least 3 people can buy a *Rail-Europ F* (family) card: the holder pays full price, the rest of the family obtain a 50% reduction in Belgium and 14 other European countries; the whole family is also entitled to a 30% reduction on Sealink and Hoverspeed Channel crossings.

Anyone under 26 years of age can purchase an *Inter-Rail* card which allows one month's unlimited 2nd-class travel within Europe.

When to Go

From the coast inland to Brussels, the Belgian climate is temperate maritime, similar to south-east England. The Ardennes has more continental weather, with warmer summers and colder winters. Rain can be expected at any time of year—and about every other day.

Average daytime temperatures in Brussels:

	J	F	M	A	M	J	J	A	S	O	N	D
Temperature °F	41	43	50	55	66	70	74	72	68	57	46	41
°C	5	6	10	13	19	21	23	22	20	14	8	6

Planning Your Budget

To give you an idea of what to expect, here's a list of average prices in Belgian francs (BF). They can only be approximate, however, as inflation creeps relentlessly up.

Airport transfers. Train (2nd class) to centre BF 70, taxi BF 630 from Central Station.

Baby-sitters. BF 200 per hour.

Bicycle hire. BF 100 per day (from railway stations).

Buses, trams and metro. Single ticket BF 35, card of 10 tickets BF 220.

Camping. BF 200–350 for a family of 4 for one night.

Car hire. *Opel Corsa LS* BF 1,400 per day, BF 14 per km., BF 12,000 per week with unlimited mileage. *Ford Sierra GL* BF 2,200 per day, BF 22 per km., BF 18,000 per week with unlimited mileage. *BMW 5201* BF 3,000 per day, BF 30 per km., BF 24,000 per week with unlimited mileage. Add 25% tax.

Cigarettes. BF 67–77 for a packet of 20/25.

Entertainment. Cinema BF 200 (cheaper on Mondays), ballet/opera BF 550–2,000, discotheque/nightclub BF 200–300 and up.

Guides. BF 2,200–2,800 per half day (3 hours), BF 3,900–5,000 (plus lunch) per day. Interpreters BF 13,900 per day.

Hairdressers. *Man's* haircut, shampoo and styling BF 550–650. *Woman's* cut and blow dry BF 1,000–1,250, shampoo and set BF 350–450, shampoo and blow-dry BF 400–480, colour rinse BF 485–755.

Hotels (double room with bath and breakfast, per night). Luxury BF 6,000–9,000, moderate BF 4,000–5,000, budget BF 1,600–2,600. *Youth hostels* BF 340–550 plus sheet rental per night with breakfast.

Meals and drinks. Breakfast BF 70–130, lunch BF 250–325, "typical" dinner (steak, French fries, salad) BF 450–600, bottle of wine BF 350–500, beer BF 35–50, soft drink BF 35–45, coffee BF 38–55.

Shopping. Hand-made lace handkerchief BF 395–595, Belgian chocolates per kilo BF 780–880.

Taxi. Meter charge BF 85, plus BF 31 per km.

Tours. Group tour of Brussels centre (half day) BF 550–600, boat tour of Port of Antwerp BF 300.

Trains. Ostend–Brussels (2nd class, one way) BF 340, Brussels–Antwerp BF 145, Brussels–Bruges BF 285.

An A–Z Summary of Practical Information and Facts

> A star (*) following an entry indicates that relevant prices are to be found on page 104.
>
> Listed after certain important terms are the appropriate French and Flemish translations, usually in the singular. A number of phrases in French (heavy type) and Flemish (italics) have also been included to help you when seeking assistance.

AIRPORT *(aéroport/luchthaven)*. Brussels National Airport at Zaventem, 12 kilometres north-east of the capital, has the customary amenities, including duty-free shops (after passport control), a tourist information/hotel reservation service (in the arrival area) and chapels and worship areas for all major faiths. Rental baggage trolleys are plentiful, porters scarce. To hire a trolley, you'll need Belgian franc coins. Change machines are provided. Left-luggage (baggage-check) lockers are available in the arrival area (near the post office).

Ground transport*. Belgium proudly claims to have been the first country in the world to build a direct rail link between its national airport and the capital. Signs guide you down to the underground platform from which trains depart for Gare du Nord and Gare Centrale in Brussels from about 6 a.m. to midnight. Purchase your ticket at the station or at the tourist information office in the baggage claim hall. The trip takes less than 20 minutes.

Infrequent city bus service connects Zaventem with the Gare du Nord.

Taxis line up in front of the airport building. The trip to the centre of town will cost you quite a bit more than the train fare.

Special Sabena buses connect Brussels Airport with Liège, Ghent Antwerp and Hasselt/Maastricht.

Flight information. For enquiries about arriving and departing flights, call 720 71 67 (for Sabena and cooperating airlines).

BABY-SITTERS* *(garde d'enfants/baby-sitter)*. The majority of hotels welcome and cater for babies and small children, providing facilities such as cots, high chairs, special food and sometimes recreation rooms.

B   If your hotel does not have its own list of contacts for baby-sitting, it will usually turn to a reliable agency. A favourite source in Brussels for sitters speaking foreign languages is the university placement office; telephone 647 23 85 on weekdays.

| Can you get me a baby-sitter for tonight? | **Pouvez-vous me trouver une baby-sitter pour ce soir?** | *Kunt u mij voor vanavond een baby-sitter bezorgen?* |

BICYCLE and MOPED HIRE*. Steep hills, heavy traffic and inadequate cycle paths in the centre of Brussels will deter most would-be pedallers, but the suburban Forêt de Soignes offers many safe bicycle paths through scenic woods. The yellow pages lists outlets under *Bicyclettes & cyclomoteurs/Fietsen & bromfietsen* (bicycles and mopeds). *Location* means hire.

Serviceable bikes—fitted with gears in hilly districts—can be hired at about 60 strategically selected railway stations throughout the country. Rail travellers are given priority and reduced rates (show your train ticket). Phone ahead to the station to make your reservation—telephone numbers and further details are given in Belgian National Railways' brochure *Train + vélo/Trein + fiets*.

Unlike the Netherlands, the bicycle is not king of the road here, and cycle paths vary widely in availability and quality. The best-equipped areas are Antwerp and West Flanders provinces.

| I'd like to hire a bicycle. | **J'aimerais louer une bicyclette.** | *Ik zou graag een fiets huren.* |

C   **CAMPING***. Belgium has more than 300 government-licensed campsites, graded in four categories. Most are located in the Ardennes and along the coast, but there are some sites in other parts of the country, a few within striking distance of the capital. Ask the Belgian National Tourist Office for its free camping brochure.

In some areas, particularly along the coast, camping is only permitted on recognized sites. Elsewhere, local farmers will often give you permission to pitch a tent or draw up a caravan (trailer) on their land for the night.

| May we camp on your land, please? | **Pouvons-nous camper sur votre terrain, s'il vous plaît?** | *Mogen wij op uw terrain kamperen, alstublieft?* |

CAR HIRE* *(location de voitures/autoverhuring).* See also DRIVING.
International and local rental firms are detailed in Brussels' yellow
pages. The best known have desks at the airport. Personnel usually
speak English. Your home driving licence will be accepted provided
you have held it for at least a year. The minimum age limit varies
generally between 20 and 25, depending on the company and the cat-
egory of vehicle you wish to hire. However, some smaller cars are
available for 18-year olds.

A credit card is by far the preferred means of payment. Collision
insurance with the first 30,000 francs deductible is available but
expensive. Collision damage waivers and personal accident policies
are available on request. There is no extra charge if you have the car
delivered to your hotel in Brussels.

CIGARETTES, CIGARS, TOBACCO* *(cigarettes; cigares; tabac/
sigaretten; sigaren; tabak).* Foreign and domestic cigarettes, about
equally priced, can be purchased at tobacconists', news-stands, super-
markets, cafés, bars and restaurants. For a typical local smoke, you
might like to try the dark *Bastos, Belga, St. Michel* or similar brands,
sold in packets of 20 or 25—but most foreigners find these cigarettes
rather rough.

Connoisseurs appreciate Belgian cigars from the Antwerp region
which, they claim, compare favourably with the more vaunted products from north of the border.

Smoking is prohibited in public buildings. Fines are heavy.

A packet of .../	**Un paquet de .../**	*Een pakje .../*
A box of matches,	**Une boîte d'allumet-**	*Een doosje lucifers,*
please.	**tes, s'il vous plaît.**	*alstublieft.*

CLOTHING. While business people and the host of national and
international civil servants in Brussels maintain a certain formality of
dress, tourists need not be affected by this. Open-necked shirts and
jeans are as popular here as anywhere. Only in the evenings, at better
restaurants and hotels, are men required to wear a jacket (not neces-
sarily a tie) and women usually dress up. Don't forget to take along a
sweater or jacket for summer evenings. Warm clothing is essential in
winter, and rainwear may be needed at any time of year.

If you go shopping for clothing or footwear in Belgium, you'll find
yourself zigzagging between French, German, English—and Belgian
—systems of measurement, depending on the shop and article. Just
ask the salesperson to size you up.

C COMMUNICATIONS

Post offices are separate from telephone and telegraph offices. Look for the words *POSTES/POSTERIJEN* in shiny white letters on a red background. Opening hours vary (see HOURS section). You may also purchase stamps at many news-stands, hotel lobbies, bookshops, street kiosks and from vending machines. Mail boxes are red and generally wall-mounted.

Poste restante (general delivery). If you're not sure where you'll be staying, have your mail sent to you *poste restante/poste-restante,* in care of the main post office in town *(poste principale/hoofdpostkontoor).* For Brussels, the full address would be:

> Mr. John Smith
> Poste Restante
> Centre
> B-1000 Brussels

You'll have to show your passport and pay a nominal sum to retrieve mail.

Telephone. Larger towns have at least one *Téléphone-Télégraphe/ Telefoon-Telegraaf* (TT) office. In Brussels, TT offices are conveniently located at 17, boulevard de l'Impératrice (near Gare Centrale), at 2, rue Henri Maus (next to the Bourse), at 1, av. Fonsny (at the Gare du Midi) and at the airport.

Away from your hotel, the TT office is the place to go to make intercontinental calls or to send telegrams and telexes.

Public telephone booths can be found at railway stations, post offices, in department stores and in the street. Those decorated with European national flags on the outside can be used for direct-dialling international calls to most Western European countries. Instructions are posted in English, Dutch, French and German. Go armed with a large stock of 5- or 20-franc pieces. Many telephone booths operate with electronic cards called "Telecard", easier to handle than coins. They can be purchased from post offices, news-stands and *libraries*.

If you are looking for a particular service, consult the yellow pages *(pages d'or/gouden gids),* published for all Belgian telephone districts. At the beginning of each volume you'll find indexes in English, Dutch, French and German.

The area code for Brussels, including the airport, is 02. You won't need it if dialling a local number from within the Brussels area.

Telegrams and telexes. During working hours, telegrams and telexes can be sent from most post offices, hotels, phone centres and railway stations. To send telegrams at night, on weekends or holidays, go to the Gare du Midi at 1, av. Fonsny. You can also send telegrams by telephone by dialling 1325.

Have you any mail for ...?	**Avez-vous du courrier pour ...?**	*Hebt u post voor ...?*
A stamp for this letter/postcard, please.	**Un timbre pour cette lettre/carte postale, s'il vous plaît.**	*Een postzegel voor deze brief/briefkaart, alstublieft.*
airmail	**par avion**	*luchtpost*
registered	**recommandé**	*aangetekend*
Can you get me this number in ...?	**Pouvez-vous me donner ce numéro à ...?**	*Kunt u mij verbinden met dit nummer in ...?*

CONVERTER CHARTS. For fluid and distance measures, see page 111. Belgium uses the metric system.

Temperature

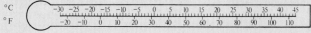

Length

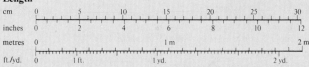

Weight

grams 0   100   200   300   400   500   600   700   800   900   1 kg
ounces 0   4   8   12   1 lb   20   24   28   2 lb.

CRIME and THEFT. Standard precautions are in order in this generally unalarming city—deposit valuables and unneeded documents in your hotel safe, remove anything from your car that may tempt thieves and lock it.

Pickpockets are a fact of life by the Grand-Place, the Bourse and at the Sunday market near Gare du Midi, where police loud-hail warnings to the throngs of shoppers.

C   The sordid red-light district near Gare du Nord has its own risks after dark. See also POLICE.

I wish to report a theft.	**Je veux signaler un vol.**	*Ik wil aangifte doen van een diefstal.*

D   **DRIVING.** To bring your car into Belgium you'll need:

- Your home driving licence *(permis de conduire/rijbewijs)* or an international driving licence
- Car registration papers *(permis de circulation/kentekenbewijs)* and certificate of ownership, if available.
- Green Card or equivalent supplementary insurance making your policy valid for foreign countries.

You must have a national identity sticker visible on the back of the car, a fire extinguisher and a red warning triangle for use in case of breakdown. Drivers and front-seat passengers are required by law to wear seat belts. Children under 12 are not allowed in the front seat.

Roads and regulations. Drive on the right and pass on the left. At junctions, cars coming from the right have priority unless you are on a main road (marked with a sign displaying a yellow diamond). Trams have priority at all times. When driving at night, headlights, not parking lights, must be used in town. Your horn should only be used in case of emergency. Alcohol limit is 80 mg/100 ml.

   Superb, toll-free motorways, illuminated at night, crisscross the country. These are designated as E roads (E411, E19, etc.).

Speed limits are 120 kilometres per hour on motorways, 90 kph on other roads and 60 kph in towns.

Traffic police, accidents. You can't mistake patrol cars—white with a broad orange or blue stripe across the top from front to back, surmounted by a blue light. Increasingly, unmarked cars are being used as well. If you need the help of the traffic police, call 101 nationwide. Phone 101 or 100 for an ambulance.

Breakdowns. Three organizations handle breakdowns on the road:

Touring Club de Belgique, tel. (02) 233 22 11

Royal Automobile Club de Belgique, tel. (02) 736 59 59
Vlaamse Automobilistenbond (based in Antwerp), tel. (03) 252 62 70

Emergency call boxes are located at regular intervals along motorways.

Fuel and oil. Filling stations are plentiful, selling *super, normale/normaal, sans plomb/loodvrij* (lead-free) and *gasoil/diesel*. Watch for signs marked "–30 cts", "–90 cts", etc. The station displaying the sign is selling petrol (gas) below the official recommended price by the amount indicated.

Parking. On the street, always park in the direction of moving traffic. Most Belgian cities have multi-storey car parks. Street parking arrangements vary. Signs marked 1–15 and 16–31 and bisected by a red slash mean that parking is not permitted on that side of the road on the dates noted. The Roman figures I and II indicate alternate-side of the street parking on odd- and even-numbered days respectively. The blue zones require a special parking disk, available at garages, bookshops and news-stands.

Fluid measures

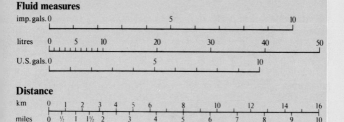

Distance

Road signs. Most road signs are the standard pictographs used throughout Europe, but you may encounter these written signs as well:

French	English	Flemish
Accotements non stabilisés	Soft shoulders	*Zachte berm*
Attention	Caution	*Opgepast*
Autres directions	Other directions	*Andere richtingen*
Chaussée déformée/ dégradée	Bad road surface	*Beschadigd wegdek*
Déviation	Diversion (detour)	*Wegomlegging*
Passage difficile	Obstruction ahead	*Moeilijke doorgang*
Péage	Toll	*Tol*
Ralentir	Slow	*Langzaam rijden*
Rappel	Reminder	*Herhaling*

D

| Sens unique | One-way street | *Eenrichtingverkeer* |
| Toutes directions | All directions | *Alle richtingen* |

Are we on the right road for ...?	**Sommes-nous sur la route de ...?**	*Zijn wij op de juiste weg naar ...?*
Fill the tank, please.	**Le plein, s'il vous plaît.**	*Vol, graag.*
Check the oil/tires/ battery.	**Veuillez contrôler l'huile/les pneus/ la batterie.**	*Kijkt u even de olie/ banden/accu na.*
I've had a break-down.	**Ma voiture est en panne.**	*Ik heb autopech.*

E **ELECTRIC CURRENT.** All of Belgium is on 220-volt, 50-cycle A.C.

EMBASSIES and CONSULATES *(ambassades; consulats/ambassades; consulaten).* Diplomatic representations are grouped in the telephone directory under the above headings. Embassies in Brussels include the following:

Australia:	6, rue Guimard, tel. 231 05 00
Canada:	2, avenue de Tervuren, tel. 735 60 40
Eire:	19–21, rue Luxembourg, tel. 513 66 33
New Zealand:	47, boulevard du Régent, tel. 512 10 40
South Africa:	26, rue de la Loi, tel. 230 68 45
U.K.	(consular department): 28, rue Joseph II, tel. 217 90 000
U.S.A.	(consular section): 25, boulevard du Régent, tel. 513 38 30

EMERGENCIES *(urgence/noodgeval).* The three-digit emergency phone numbers are valid throughout Belgium. Other numbers are for Brussels only.

Accidents/Fire brigade	100
Ambulance (Belgian Red Cross)	100, 101, 649 50 10
Dentist (evenings and weekends)	426 10 26
Doctor (24 hours)	648 80 00
Pharmacy (evenings and weekends)	479 18 18
Police, gendarmerie, emergency	101

In Brussels, you can phone 6484014 for general advice in English round the clock ("Help Line").

I need a doctor/ dentist.	**Il me faut un méde-cin/un dentiste.**	*Ik heb een arts/een tandarts nodig.*
hospital	**hôpital**	*ziekenhuis*

ENTRY FORMALITIES and CUSTOMS. Most visitors, including nationals of Australia, Canada, Eire, New Zealand, the U.K. and U.S.A., need only a valid passport (no visa) to enter Belgium. British subjects can travel on the simplified Visitor's Passport.

The following chart shows what main duty-free items you may take into Belgium and, when returning home, into your own country:

Into:	Cigarettes		Cigars		Tobacco	Spirits	Wine
Belgium 1)	300	or	75	or	400 g.	1.5 l. and 5 l.	
2)	200	or	50	or	250 g.	1 l. and 2 l.	
Australia	200	or	250 g. or		250 g.	1 l. or 1 l.	
Canada	200	and	50	and	900 g.	1.1 l. or 1.1 l.	
N.Zealand	200	or	50	or	250 g.	1 l. and 4.5 l.	
S.Africa	400	and	50	and	250 g.	1 l. and 2 l.	
U.K.*	200	or	50	or	250 g.	1 l. and 2 l.	
U.S.A.	200	and	100	and	**	1 l. or 1 l.	

1) non-tax-free goods bought in EEC countries
2) goods bought outside EEC countries or tax-free goods bought in EEC countries

* For items purchased in a duty-free shop.
** No restriction for personal use only.

Currency restrictions. There are no limitations on the import or export of either local or foreign currencies.

I've nothing to declare.	**Je n'ai rien à déclarer.**	*Ik heb niets aan te geven.*
It's for my personal use.	**C'est pour mon usage personnel.**	*Het is voor eigen gebruik.*

G **GUIDES and INTERPRETERS*** *(guide; interprète/gids; tolk).* Most city sightseeing tours and excursions are accompanied by a multilingual guide. Before purchasing your ticket, ask to make sure that English is offered. Tourist offices can supply guides for private purposes if you order in advance.

In the very international city of Brussels, interpreters and translators abound—consult the yellow pages.

H **HAIRDRESSERS*** *(coiffeur/kapper).* Larger hotels have their own salons, and others can easily be found. There are no hairdressing facilities at Brussels airport. Prices vary widely, depending on whether you go to a chic hair stylist or a backstreet barber.

haircut	**coupe**	*knippen*
shampoo and set	**shampooing et mise en plis**	*wassen en watergolven*
blow dry	**brushing**	*föhnen*

HEALTH and MEDICAL CARE. Medical care is of the highest standard but expensive, so it's worth making sure that your normal health insurance covers foreign journeys. British nationals enjoy reduced-rate treatment in case of injury or accident in Belgium. Many doctors speak English.

You need have no fear of drinking the tap water—but leave street fountains strictly to the birds.

Chemists' *(pharmacie/apotheek)* are easily recognized by a green cross. A few pharmacies stay open in each neighbourhood after hours. The list is posted outside each one and published in the weekend editions of the local newspapers.

Where's the duty pharmacy?	**Où est la pharmacie de garde?**	*Waar is de dienstdoende apotheek?*

HITCH-HIKING *(auto-stop/liften).* Allowed everywhere except motorways. You're likely to do better if you write your destination on a hand-held sign in both French and Flemish. See PLACE NAMES.

International Lifeservice brings together drivers and hikers. Information from TAXISTOP, Onderbergen 51, 9000 Ghent, tel. (091) 23 23 10.

Can you give me a lift to ...?	**Pouvez-vous m'emmener à ...?**	*Kunt u mij een lift geven naar ...?*

114

HOTELS and ACCOMMODATION*. The Belgian National Tourist Office puts out an annual guide to hotels.

The hotels of Brussels cover the usual spectrum from luxurious and expensive to simple and cheap. In the absence of an official grading system, the capital's tourist office issues a list of approved hotels, presented according to price and facilities. These hotels display a special shield. Room rates must be posted at the reception desk and in each room.

For hotel rooms in Brussels, you can reserve through the two tourist offices (see p. 123).

You can book hotel rooms in advance, anywhere in Belgium, through a free service offered by Belgique Tourisme Réservations.

Write to

BTR, P.O. Box 41, 1000 Brussels 23 (tel. 02-230 50 29).

Apartments, bungalows and villas (furnished) can be rented for a holiday period, particularly in Brussels, the Ardennes and along the coast. Write to the local tourist office for full information.

Farmhouse arrangements are becoming increasingly popular—again, particularly on coastal regions and the Ardennes. Ask for the national tourist office's special brochure *Budget Holidays*.

Youth and student accommodation is available in both town and country. Some addresses are featured in the *Budget Holidays* brochure mentioned above, but for full details contact your national student travel organization or youth hostel association.

a double/single room	**une chambre à deux lits/à un lit**	*een tweepersoonskamer/eenpersoonskamer*
with/without bath	**avec/sans bains**	*met/zonder bad*
What's the rate per night?	**Quel est le tarif pour une nuit?**	*Hoeveel kost het per nacht?*

HOURS. All hours given here must be regarded as approximate, since schedules—even for public services such as the post office—vary considerably.

Banks are generally open from 9 a.m. to 3.30 or 4 p.m. non-stop, Monday to Friday. A few are open Saturday morning. Some banks are open until 6 p.m. two days a week. Small branches may close for lunch.

H **Currency exchange offices** at Brussels airport open from 7 a.m. to 9.45 p.m. and those at Gare du Midi and Gare du Nord operate from 7 a.m. to 10.45 p.m. every day of the year. The office at Gare Centrale is open from 8 a.m. to 9 p.m. every day.

Museums. 10 a.m. to 5 p.m., Tuesday to Sunday, sometimes with a one-hour lunchtime closure between noon and 2 p.m. Closed on Mondays and public holidays.

Office and business hours normally run from 9 a.m. to 5 p.m., Monday to Friday.

Post offices. Hours are normally from 9 a.m. to 5 p.m. The post office at Gare du Midi (48a, avenue de Fonsny) is open 24 hours a day, every day of the year. Smaller offices, particularly on country areas, may take a lunchtime break and also close earlier in the afternoon.

Shops. Department stores generally do business from 9.15 or 9.30 a.m. to 6.30 p.m. six days a week, closing late one evening (Friday in Brussels). Smaller shops may close over lunch and stay open later in the evening.

Telephone/telegraph offices. The office at the Gare du Midi at 1, av. Fonsny is open 24 hours every day.

L **LANGUAGE.** Belgium's troublesome linguistic division stems in part from its historic position on the ancient boundary between the Roman and Germanic worlds. Nowadays, about 57% of the country (the northern half) speaks Flemish—or Dutch, which is the modern, written form of the language. French is the language in Wallonia, southern Belgium, and a small percentage of the people in eastern districts speak German.

In Brussels, an officially bilingual enclave in Dutch-speaking territory, about 80% of the native population are French-speakers. But you will also find that English is widely spoken in this European capital.

Belgian French is virtually the same as that spoken in France, but the Walloons say *septante* and *nonante* instead of *soixante-dix* and *quatre-vingt-dix* (seventy and ninety).

Assuming that their language is a mystery to most foreigners, Dutch-speakers will readily converse in whatever bits of languages they know. But they'll also appreciate your efforts to master at least a few basic expressions.

The Berlitz phrase books FRENCH FOR TRAVELLERS and DUTCH FOR TRAVELLERS cover most situations you're likely to encounter in your travels in Belgium. See also the Berlitz French-English/English-French and Dutch-English/English-Dutch pocket dictionaries, each containing a glossary of 12,500 terms plus a menu-reader supplement.

A few words to get you going:

Good morning	**Bonjour**	*Goedemorgen*
Good afternoon	**Bonjour**	*Goedemiddag*
Good evening	**Bonsoir**	*Goedenavond*
Goodbye	**Au revoir**	*Tot ziens*
Please	**S'il vous plaît**	*Alstublieft*
Thank you	**Merci**	*Dank u*
How do you do?	**Enchanté.**	*Prettig om kennis met u te maken.*
Do you speak English?	**Parlez-vous anglais?**	*Spreekt u Engels?*

LAUNDRY and DRY-CLEANING *(blanchisserie; nettoyage à sec* or *teinturier/wasserij; stomerij)*. Establishments can be found in all parts of town, some of which (like the larger hotels) offer same-day service. They are all listed in the Brussels yellow pages. For a more economical wash, try a laundromat *(salon-lavoir/wasserette* or *wassalon)*.

When will it be ready?	**Quand est-ce que ce sera prêt?**	*Wanneer is het klaar?*
I must have it for tomorrow morning	**Il me le faut pour demain matin.**	*Ik heb dit morgenvroeg nodig.*

LOST PROPERTY. If retracing your steps brings no luck, your first line of inquiry, anywhere in Belgium, would generally be through the police. In Brussels, phone the *service des objets trouvés/gevonden voorwerpen)* at 517 98 65.

Other lost property offices:
Airport: tel. 720 59 80
Railway: at Gare du Quartier Léopold, tel. 218 60 50, ext. 6267 (after one week)
Public transport: located in the Porte de Namur *métro* station, tel. 515 23 94, from 9.30 a.m. to 12.30 p.m.
Taxi drivers would normally hand in goods left in their vehicles to either the police or their head office.

L	I've lost my …	**J'ai perdu mon …**	*Ik ben mijn … kwijt.*
	wallet	**portefeuille**	*portefeuille*
	handbag	**sac à main**	*handtas*
	passport	**passeport**	*paspoort*

M   **MAPS.** Local tourist offices and hotels hand out simplified street-plans adequate for general sightseeing purposes. Excellent maps are on sale in bookshops for detailed exploration of the countryside, and the main cities are well catered for by fold-out or pocketbook-type publications. Streets-plans of Brussels may be bilingual or in French or Flemish only. Falk-Verlag, Hamburg, which prepared the maps for this book, produces comprehensive, indexed street-plans of Brussels and other major Belgian cities.

a street plan of Brussels	**un plan de Bruxelles**	*een plattegrond van Brussel*

MEETING PEOPLE. Muster your school French or dabble in Dutch, and you'll find that taxi drivers, bar-hoppers and anyone else you come in contact with will appreciate your efforts and respond. On the other hand, it won't take you long to meet a resident English-speaker in Brussels' cosmopolitan world. Cafés (especially in the Ixelles area), discos, English-language churches and, in fine weather, the capital's outdoor tavern terraces are the easiest places to meet people. In addition, some restaurants have special "conversation tables".

In shops, restaurants, on the telephone or wherever, always start off with a polite word of greeting (see Language). A lot of hand-shaking takes place on social occasions.

MONEY MATTERS

Currency. The unit of Belgian currency is the *franc* (called bys this name in both French and Dutch), abbreviated BF or FB. It is divided into 100 centimes. Coins in circulation: 50 centimes, 1, 5, 20 and 50 francs, banknotes: 50, 100, 1000 and 5000 francs.

Belgian currency, at parity with the Luxembourg franc, circulates freely in the Grand Duchy; Luxembourg francs, though always accepted, are not very popular in Belgium. Watch out for them in your change.

Banks *(banque/bank)* and **currency exchange offices** *(bureau de change/wisselkantoor)*. Plentiful in city centres, seaside resorts, at railway stations and at the airport, these give a better rate than hotels, shops and restaurants. In the Brussels area, some currency exchange facilities are open on Sundays and public holidays. See Hours section. There are currency exchange machines at the airport which make transactions in four currencies.

Traveller's cheques *(chèque de voyage/reischeque)* are widely accepted throughout Belgium. When you change traveller's cheques, a standard, flat-rate minimum charge is made for any amount, so don't cash them in dribs and drabs. Take your passport along when you go to change money.

Eurocheques are accepted by a wide range of businesses, including motorway filling stations.

Credit cards *(carte de crédit/credit card)* may be used in many hotels, restaurants, shops, petrol stations, etc. Signs are posted indicating which cards are accepted.

Sales tax, service charge. Called *TVA/BTW,* a sales (value-added) tax is imposed on almost all goods and services. In hotels and restaurants, this is accompanied by a service charge. The sign *"Service et TVA inclus/Service en BTW inbegrepen"* tells you that services and *TVA/BTW* are included in the price. Enquire if you are eligible for a TVA refund on more expensive purchases.

I want to change some pounds/dollars.	**Je voudrais changer des livres sterling/ dollars.**	*Ik wil graag ponden/ dollars wisselen.*
Do you accept traveller's cheques?	**Acceptez-vous les chèques de voyage?**	*Accepteert u reis-cheques?*
Can I pay with this credit card?	**Puis-je payer avec cette carte de crédit?**	*Kan ik met deze credit card betalen?*

NEWSPAPERS and MAGAZINES *(journal; revue/krant; tijdschrift).*

Leading foreign newspapers and magazines are available at shops and new-stands in the centre of Brussels and other large cities. The British press is particularly well represented, and Americans will be able to keep up to date with the Paris-based *International Herald Tribune* and Brussels-edited *Wall Street Journal/Europe.*

For an English-language round-up of local activities and events, buy *The Bulletin.*

Have you any English-language newspapers?	**Avez-vous des jour-naux en anglais?**	*Heeft u Engelse kranten?*

P PHOTOGRAPHY. All types of film are widely available, and developing and printing are of high quality. Processing can be done in one hour or less. Enlargements take a day. All airport security machines use X-rays, which can ruin your film on repeated exposure. If worried, enclose it in a film-shield.

To avoid frustration, try to arrange your photographic sessions with the following in mind:

Morning sunlight falls on Notre-Dame de la Chapelle, Grand-Place (west side), Palais de Justice and Porte de Hal.

Afternoon sunlight falls on Notre-Dame du Sablon, the house of the Dukes of Brabant and the façade of Cathédral St-Michel.

Many monuments are illuminated at night.

Using a flash is forbidden in many museums, and in some cameras are banned altogether. Check with the attendant.

I'd like a film for this camera.	**J'aimerais un film pour cet appareil.**	*Mag ik een film voor dit toestel?*
How long will it take to develop this film?	**Combien de temps faut-il pour développer ce film?**	*Hoe lang duurt het ont-wikkelen van deze film?*

PLACE NAMES. The place name puzzle baffles every first-time visitor to Belgium. Dozens of towns bear different names in French and Flemish, but in most parts of the country road signs are only in the language of the region you are in. Below is a list of some important equivalents (with the official name given first).

Aalst/Alost	**Liège**/Luik
Antwerpen/Anvers	**Mechelen**/Malines
Arlon/Aarlen	**Mons**/Bergen
Brugge/Bruges	**Namur**/Namen
De Haan/Le Coq	**Oostende**/Ostende
Dendermonde/Termonde	**Oudenaarde**/Audenarde
De Panne/La Panne	**Roeselare**/Roulers
Gent/Gand	**Ronse**/Renaix
Geraardsbergen/Grammont	**Soignies**/Zinnik
Huy/Hoei	**Tienen**/Tirlemont
Ieper/Ypres	**Tongeren**/Tongres
Koksijde/Coxyde	**Tournai**/Doornik
Kortrijk/Courtrai	**Wavre**/Waver
Leuven/Louvain	**Zoutleeuw**/Léau

POLICE. Belgium has more guardians of the law in proportion to its population than any other EEC country. The "men in blue" come in two varieties: the municipal *police/politie* and the *gendarmerie/rijk-swacht.*

As a rule, the police are the ones you turn to for information or assistance, while the gendarmerie deal with large-scale operations such as crowd control, traffic supervision and road patrol. Both can be reached by dialling 101.

Where's the nearest police station?	**Où est le commissariat de police le plus proche?**	*Waar is het dichtsbijzijnde politiebureau?*

PUBLIC HOLIDAYS *(jour férié/openbare feestdag).* The following public holidays are observed throughout the country:

Jan. 1	New Year's Day	*Jour de l'An / Nieuwjaar*
May 1	Labour Day	*Fête du Travail / Dag van de arbeid*
July 21	National Day	*Fête Nationale / Nationale feestdag*
Aug. 15	Assumption	*Assomption / Maria Hemelvaart*
Nov. 1	All Saints' Day	*Toussaint / Allerheiligen*
Nov. 11	Armistice Day	*Anniversaire de l'Armistice / Wapenstilstand*
Dec. 25	Christmas Day	*Noël / Kerstdag*
Movable:	Easter Monday	*Lundi de Pâques / Paasmaandag*
	Ascension	*Ascension / Hemelvaartsdag*
	Whit Monday	*Lundi de Pentecôte / Pinkstermaandag*

If a holiday falls on a Sunday, the following Monday is taken off instead.

RADIO and TELEVISION. If your hotel room has a television, chances are you'll be thoroughly spoiled. Belgian cable TV feeds as many as 21 stations in most sets. Domestic telecasts are in both French and Dutch, and the bonus programmes come from Britain (BBC 1 and BBC 2), France, Germany, Luxembourg and, frequently in English, the Netherlands, but not CNN yet.

You'll be able to listen to English-language stations on your hotel radio or any portable one. Broadcasts include the U.S. Armed Forces Network on 101.7 FM and the BBC World Service on 648 medium wave/AM.

R   **RELIGIOUS SERVICES** *(office religieux/kerkdienst)*. Though Belgium is a predominantly Roman Catholic country, Protestant denominations are quite well represented. You can attend English services at many churches in Brussels. There are mosques and synagogues, but services are not in English. Inquire at your hotel reception desk.

T   **TIME DIFFERENCE.** The following chart shows the time difference between Belgium and various cities in winter. Between April and September, Belgian clocks are put forward one hour:

New York	London	**Belgium**	Jo'burg	Sydney	Auckland
6 a.m.	11 a.m.	**noon**	1 p.m.	10 p.m.	midnight

TIPPING. Service charge is included in hotel and restaurant bills. However, it's appropriate to tip bellboys, maids, etc., for their services. Some suggestions:

Barber	20%
Cinema usher	BF 10 per person
Hairdresser	included
Lavatory attendant	BF 10–15
Maid, per week	BF 100–150
Hotel porter, per bag	BF 30
Taxi driver	included
Tourist guide	10%
Waiter	optional

TOILETS. Public conveniences can be found in the larger *métro* and railway stations, museums and department stores. If there's an attendant on duty, you should leave a tip. The rare and less-than-salubrious street facilities are best avoided.

If toilet doors are not marked with the usual silhouettes, you'll see the inscriptions *WC, Toilettes/Toiletten, Dames* (ladies) and *Messieurs/Heren* (gentlemen).

Where are the toilets?	**Où sont les toilettes?**	*Waar zijn de toiletten?*

TOURIST INFORMATION OFFICES. Branches of the Belgian National Tourist Office will be of great help in planning your trip.

U.K: 38 Dover Street, London W1X 3RB, tel. (01) 499 5379
U.S.A.: 745 Fifth Avenue, New York, NY 10022, tel. (212) 758-8130

Headquarters of the Belgian National Tourist Office is located at 61, rue du Marché aux Herbes, 1000 Brussels, tel. (02) 512 30 30

The Tourist and Information Office of Brussels, T.I.B., is situated in the Town Hall *(Hôtel de Ville)* at
Grand-Place, 1000 Brussels, tel. (02) 513 89 40.

There is an information centre for arriving passengers at the airport in the baggage claim area.

In virtually all Belgian towns you'll find a tourist office near the railway station or central square. Signs to look for:

French	*Flemish*
Office du tourisme	Verkeersbureau
Syndicat d'initiative	Informatiebureau
Renseignements	Inlichtingen

Where is the tourist office?	**Où est l'office du tourisme?**	*Waar is het verkeers-bureau?*

TRANSPORT*. The Brussels public transport system is an integrated network of underground (subway), tram (streetcar) and bus routes providing excellent coverage of the capital and immediate surroundings. Free route maps are available at the tourist offices, at S.T.I.B. *(Société des Transports Intercommunaux de Bruxelles)* underground information centres at Porte de Namur, Rogier and Gare du Midi, and at the S.T.I.B. office at av. Toison d'Or, 15.

The **underground** *(métro/metro)* consists of a line crossing the city from the east to the west and a new north/south link. Stations are indicated by a large blue M sign, and decorated inside with paintings, sculpture, ceramics—tapestries even (see p. 39).

Trams serve the whole city and link up usefully with the *métro;* these lines are called the *pré-métro/premetro.*

Buses are of two kinds. Yellow and blue/yellow (extra long) ones operate only within the city limits, orange/yellow ones go out to the suburbs. All-night buses *(bus de nuit/nachtbus)* provide skeleton

T service on a limited number of routes. All stops are "on request" *(Arrêt sur demande/Halte op verzoek)*—to board the vehicle, make a sign with the hand; to get off, push the button.

Individual tickets and 5-ride tickets, allowing you up to an hour's travel on any combination of tram, bus and *métro* within the city limits, can be purchased on buses and trams and in *métro* stations. Ten-trip tickets are also available. Keep your ticket until you complete your journey.

With a "Go as you please" ticket you have the run of the public transport system (bus, metro, tram but not trains) for a whole day in any of 25 Belgian cities and towns. You can buy them at *métro* stations, at S.T.I.B. information offices (see p. 123), at the tourist offices and at numerous newsagents.

Taxis. Cabs wait at ranks outside stations, large hotels and other key points throughout the city. You can also order them by telephone.

Taxis are metered and the price shown is all-inclusive for any number of passengers. The per-kilometre rate doubles for a Brussels-based cab once it leaves the city limits. There is no extra charge for luggage or night trips.

Trains *(train/trein)* are classed as I/C (Intercity), I/R (Inter-regional), P (Rush-hour service) and L (local) in descending order of rapidity. Tourist trains (T) provide express service during peak periods. The capital's five main railway stations are Gare du Nord for domestic and international trains and the shuttle service to the airport, Gare Centrale for domestic trains and the airport shuttle, Gare du Midi for domestic and international trains, Gare de Schaerbeek for auto trains and Gare du Quartier Léopold for domestic trains and some departures for Luxembourg.

Tourists will find the *B-Tourrail* good value. It entitles the holder to 5 days unrestricted travel within a period of 17 days anywhere in Belgium. See also pp. 102–103.

When's the next bus/ train to …?	**Quand part le prochain bus/train pour …?**	*Wanneer vertrekt de volgende bus/trein naar …?*
I want a ticket to …	**J'aimerais un billet pour …**	*Ik wil graag een kaartje naar …*
single (one way)	**aller simple**	*enkele reis*
return (round-trip)	**aller et retour**	*retour*
first/second class	**première/deuxième classe**	*eerste/tweede klas*

SOME USEFUL EXPRESSIONS

	French	*Flemish*
yes/no	**oui/non**	*ja/nee*
please	**s'il vous plaît**	*alstublieft*
thank you	**merci**	*dank u*
excuse me	**excusez-moi**	*neemt u me niet kwalijk*
where/when/how	**où/quand/comment**	*waar/wanneer/hoe*
how long	**combien de temps**	*hoe lang*
how far	**à quelle distance**	*hoe ver*
today	**aujourd'hui**	*vandaag*
yesterday/tomorrow	**hier/demain**	*gisteren/morgen*
day/week	**jour/semaine**	*dag/week*
month/year	**mois/année**	*maand/jaar*
left/right	**gauche/droite**	*links/rechts*
up/down	**en haut/en bas**	*boven/beneden*
good/bad	**bon/mauvais**	*goed/slecht*
big/small	**grand/petit**	*groot/klein*
cheap/expensive	**bon marché/cher**	*goedkoop/duur*
hot/cold	**chaud/froid**	*warm/koud*
old/new	**vieux/neuf**	*oud/nieuw*
open/closed	**ouvert/fermé**	*open/dicht*
entrance/exit	**entrée/sortie**	*entree/uitgang*
pull/push	**tirer/pousser**	*trekken/duwen*
occupied/vacant	**occupé/libre**	*bezet/vrij*
I don't understand.	**Je ne comprends pas.**	*Ik begrijp het niet.*
Please write it down.	**Veuillez bien me l'écrire.**	*Wilt u het alstublieft opschrijven?*
What does this mean?	**Que signifie ceci?**	*Wat betekent dit?*
Could you help me, please?	**Aidez-moi, s'il vous plaît.**	*Kunt u mij helpen, alstublieft?*
I'd like ...	**J'aimerais ...**	*Ik wil graag ...*
How much is it?	**C'est combien?**	*Hoeveel kost dat?*
Where's the toilet?	**Où sont les toilettes?**	*Waar zijn de toiletten?*

Index

An asterisk (*) next to a page number indicates a map reference.

127

INDEX